WILLIAM CROTCH (1775-1847)

WILLIAM CROTCH
(1775-1847)

Composer, Artist, Teacher

by

JONATHAN RENNERT

TERENCE DALTON LIMITED
LAVENHAM   SUFFOLK
1975

Published by
TERENCE DALTON LIMITED
ISBN 0 900963 61 1

Text set in 11pt Baskerville Typeface.

Printed in Great Britain at
The Lavenham Press Limited
Lavenham   Suffolk

Contents

Index of Illustrations

Acknowledgements

During the preparation of this book I have received help and advice from many people, including (in alphabetical order):

Richard Andrewes (Curator, Pendlebury Library, Cambridge),
Miss Suzanne Bernstein (New York, U.S.A.),
N.C. Buck (Assistant Librarian, St John's College, Cambridge).
Hugh Cobbe (Department of Manuscripts, British Museum),
Dr Charles Cudworth (formerly Curator, Pendlebury Library, Cambridge),
John Emlyn-Jones (London),
David Gedge (Brecon Cathedral),
(the late) John Gittins (formerly Lay-clerk, Manchester Cathedral),
George Guest (Fellow and Organist, St John's College, Cambridge, and Cambridge University Organist),
Roger Judd (Master of the Music, St Michael's College, Tenbury),
Ian Kemp (Fellow, St John's College, Cambridge),
Miss Jean M. Kennedy (County Archivist, Norfolk Record Office),
A. Hyatt King (Superintendent, British Museum Music Room),
Professor Armand W. Kitto (Evansville University, U.S.A.),
Alan Learmouth (Managing Director, Serpentine Press Limited),
Simon Lindley (Organist and Master of the Choristers, Leeds Parish Church),
Barry Lyndon (Clerk, Royal College of Organists, London),
Dr E. D. Mackerness (University of Sheffield),
Dr J.F.A. Mason (Librarian, Christ Church, Oxford),
Robert S. McDowall (Royal School of Church Music),
Charles Morgenstern (Assistant Librarian, St John's College, Oxford),
Dr Stephen Pasmore (London),
Robert Ponsonby (Controller of Music, B.B.C.),
Simon Preston (Organist, Christ Church Cathedral, Oxford),
David Robinson (Royal Academy of Music, London),
Dr Watkins Shaw (Keeper, Parry Room Library, Royal College of Music, London),

Miss Unity Sherrington (formerly Librarian, Royal College of
   Organists, London),
Mrs Lydia Smallwood (formerly Music Librarian, Rowe Library,
   King's College, Cambridge),
Dan Symonds (Librarian, Royal School of Church Music),
David B. Taylor (Lay-clerk, Christ Church Cathedral, Oxford),
Dr Nicholas Temperley (Illinois, U.S.A.),
Rodney Tibbs *(Cambridge Evening News)*,
Vicar of St Peter and St Paul, Bishop's Hull,
Cecilia Walker (Director of Music, St John's College School,
   Cambridge),
Peter Ward-Jones (Music Librarian, Bodleian Library, Oxford),
Derek Williams (Assistant Under-Librarian (Music), University
   Library, Cambridge).

Particular thanks are due to Dr Cudworth, who read the proofs
and made a number of helpful suggestions which have been incor-
porated in the text.

Jonathan Rennert, 1975

Foreword

T O MANY people the name of William Crotch conjures up visions of an unusually precocious little boy who could play a tune resembling our National Anthem (with a suitable bass) at the age of two; who gave daily organ recitals in London from the age of four; who composed an oratorio at the age of eleven; who became Organist of Christ Church, Oxford before he was fifteen, but (unlike Mozart) later failed to fulfil his quite extraordinary early promise.

To organists and members of church and chapel choirs he is the composer of the popular Epiphany anthem *Lo! star-led chiefs* and one or two chants.

To professors, staff and students of the Royal Academy of Music he is the revered and honoured first Principal (1822-1832).

But there is much more of interest about this remarkable musician, who enjoyed during his lifetime a very high reputation as organist, composer, lecturer and teacher.

It is fitting that, during the year in which we celebrate the bicentenary of the birth of William Crotch, a book should appear which contains not only a full account of his life but also an evaluation of his music.

It was while he was Organ Scholar of St John's College, Cambridge, that Jonathan Rennert first became deeply interested in William Crotch (who also had connections with that College). That interest prompted him to assemble a choir and orchestra for a public performance of the oratorio *Palestine* which he conducted himself. Since then he has performed the organ concertos and many other works by Crotch.

With detailed knowledge and practical experience behind him Jonathan Rennert is particularly well qualified to assess the value of Crotch's music and to attempt to explain why works which were so highly esteemed during the composer's life-time should now be suffering almost complete neglect.

David Willcocks

1975

William Crotch at the age of three.

CHAPTER ONE

The Infant Crotch

THE life of Doctor Crotch is, at first sight, a success story; the fascinating tale of the youngest-ever infant prodigy who grew into a brilliant man, respected by his contemporaries, though now an obscure historical figure.

The true picture is more alarming, highlighting as it does the callousness of fashionable English society in the late Georgian era. Crotch was the victim, first of ruthless exploitation, when careful guidance was needed, later of indifference, when encouragement was required.

The man who died eating a large dinner at his son's home—outwardly at one with the world—was hardened and disappointed. The man who turned, in his last bed-ridden years, more and more towards the comfort of his religious faith, had been used and then rejected by his fellow-countrymen.

The genius which can be glimpsed in his music—music which, in many cases, received only two or three performances—had been repressed and thwarted.

Crotch's father, Michael, was a little, sharp-faced man who was rarely seen without his cocked hat and red breeches. By trade he was a carpenter, though his interests ranged over a wide area, from astronomy to drawing, architecture to drama, mechanics to music. And it was his passion for music which led him to build a small pipe-organ in the dining room of the family home in Green's Lane, St George's Colgate, Norwich. On this instrument he taught himself to play his favourite psalms, as well as tunes such as *God save great George our King, Let ambition fire thy mind* and *The Easter Hymn.*

Michael Crotch lived with his second wife, Isabella (William's mother), and two sons from his first marriage, Michael Beale Crotch, a trumpeter, and John Beale Crotch. It was into this household that William was born on 5th July, 1775.

The first signs that the infant was musically inclined came when he was about eighteen months old, for whenever his father began to play the organ, he would leave whatever he was doing to listen—something which his mother found particularly frustrating if he was eating his food and just abandoned it.

Very soon he had learned to touch the first note of whichever tune he wanted his father to play, and if further explanation were needed, he would play the first two or three notes.

When he was two years and three weeks old, a visit to the house by a friend of his father's, Mrs Lulman, who sang and accompanied herself on the organ, seemed to fire William's enthusiasm to play himself. At any rate, that evening when his mother was putting him to bed, he screamed and struggled violently until she allowed him to run into the dining-room and over to the organ. He beat down the keys haphazardly with his tiny fists, while his mother good-humouredly worked the bellows.

The next morning, when Mrs Crotch had gone out, William persuaded his brother John (who was then nearly thirteen) to blow the bellows and, sitting on his knee, the infant again beat down the keys. Soon, however, he was picking out enough of the melody of God save great George our King to awaken the curiosity of his father, who was working in the garret.

He came downstairs, expecting to find John at the organ, and let out a cry of disbelief when he saw his youngest son at the keyboard. His wife was equally astounded on returning to the house and being ushered by her husband into the dining room to witness their small child's performance.

Even more amazed were they when, the following day, William added a second part beneath the melody, and the third day, he successfully attempted the bass part.

When Mr and Mrs Crotch told the tale to their neighbours, they were laughingly advised not to tell anybody else. Such a story, which must be the result of fond parental exaggeration, would expose them to ridicule if it were to be publicised and investigated.

However, a few days later, Mr Crotch was ill and unable to go out to work. The master-weaver, Mr Paul, who employed him, happened to be passing along Green's Lane and, hearing the sound of the organ coming from the Crotches' house, jumped to the conclusion that Mr Crotch had taken the day off under false pretences.

He stormed into the house, ran upstairs and flung open the door of the dining room, only to find a tiny infant playing the organ while his older brother pumped the bellows.

His reaction was to turn on his heels, rush out into the street and bring in some of the neighbours to hear the child for themselves. News spread fast, and about a hundred people arrived the following day to see for themselves the strange little two-year-old who played tunes on the organ.

Each day larger numbers of people converged from all parts of Norwich, until in desperation, the child's parents were forced to limit William's public appearances to certain days and hours.

Visitors were not content just to listen. They would play tunes for William to repeat, and melodies to which he had to add bass-lines. In both of these tests he excelled. They would also purposely play wrong notes in tunes which the child knew, and he would invariably fly into a rage, dash their hands from the keys and show them how the piece should be played.

His every whim was indulged, and he soon discovered that if he refused to play when asked, visitors would give him sweetmeats and make a fuss of him. In later life, Crotch regretted his early childhood: "I was a spoilt child," he would remember, "petted, flattered, and encouraged to be rude."

His repertory grew fast. One of the tunes he would at first play most regularly was *Let ambition fire thy mind,* but he also memorised fragments of organ voluntaries which he heard in the Cathedral; and following a visit, in November 1777, by the composer, Mr Mully, who played William a voluntary he had composed, the infant would play nothing but what he described as "the Gentleman's fine thing". Mr Mully himself, returning to the house a few days after playing the piece once to the child, confirmed that he had remembered it accurately.

A frequent caller, in these early days, was Dr Charles Burney, the musical historian, friend of George III and Queen Charlotte, and of many leading statesmen, painters, writers and musicians. His *Account of an Infant Musician* was published in the *Philosophical Transactions* of the Royal Society, alongside articles bearing such titles as *Account of the Free Martin, On the organs of speech of the Orang Outang,* and *Of the manner in which the Russians treat persons affected by the fumes of burning charcoal, and other effluvia of the same nature.*

Burney described the way in which little Crotch hardly ever looked at the keyboard when he played, and observed the strange method of fingering which the child had evolved to accommodate his small hand. His stretch was only a sixth, which caused difficulties at the end of *The Easter Hymn,* where he liked to play full chords in each hand. For fast passages, he used his knuckles, tumbling his hands over the keys.

His perfect pitch, which was accurate even at the extremes of the keyboard, was frequently tested by visitors to the house, after William's father had discovered it quite by chance. A note on the organ had ciphered, and the child had run straight to the instrument and laid his finger on the offending note. The next day Mr Crotch had purposely caused a number of notes to cipher, both individually and together, with the same result. As his ear grew more practised, William came to be able to name the notes when as many as a dozen were sounded simultaneously.

Another much-witnessed feat was his ability to transpose from one key to another. The Honourable Daines Barrington, who knew Burney and also wrote a report on the infant, remarked: "Observing this readiness in the child to transpose, I desired him to try it [*Minuet de la Cour*] in C; which he not only complied with, but proceeded regularly through the whole octave, whilst he sometimes looked back with great archness upon me, inquiring whether I knew in what key he was then playing; and having answered him once or twice wrong on purpose, he triumphed much in setting me right."

Crotch's improvisations were original but undisciplined. Often they had no regular rhythmic pulse, and never was there any hint of triple rhythm. On the other hand, his harmonic sense was more advanced, and he had some success at providing an extemporary bass against a right-hand melody played by another person on the same keyboard. Burney analysed this ability in greater detail: "He generally gives, indeed, the key-note to passages formed from its common chord and its inversions, and is quick at discovering when the fifth of the key will serve as a base. At other times he makes the third of the key serve as an accompaniment to melodies formed from the harmony of the chord to the key-note; and if simple passages are played slow, in a regular progression ascending or descending, he soon finds out that thirds or tenths, below the treble, will serve his purpose in furnishing an agreeable accompaniment."

In the summer of 1778, when her son was just three, Mrs Crotch decided that his gifts should be exhibited further afield. Accordingly, she and the young boy set off on a tour of Ipswich, Oxford, Framlingham and Bury St Edmunds. In each town, their presence would be announced by newspaper advertisements like this one: "Master Crotch, the self-taught musical child, aged three, to perform on the Piano Forte at No. 2, Saville Row, each day from twelve till two o'clock—Admittance Ladies and Gentlemen 2s."

It was on this tour that William was first introduced to a spinet, and not understanding that its mechanism differed from that of the organ, refused to play until someone had brought over a pair of bellows and started to pump them.

At Loddon the trumpet stop on the organ was so loud and so badly out-of-tune that the little organist ran out of the building, and could not be coaxed back for a full two hours. But apart from this, and a thunderstorm which interrupted his performance on the Ipswich church organ, the tour was a success.

So much so, that a second was arranged, and this time brother John joined William and his mother. Audiences in King's Lynn, Ely, Great Yarmouth and Hadleigh were able to hear the child wonder, while a third tour in October and November covered Thetford, Cambridge, Ware, Oxford and Enfield.

In each place, William was introduced to the leading local musicians—the Cathedral or church organist, and (in Cambridge) the Professor of Music, Dr Randall, and the violin virtuoso, Giardini. Then there was an organ builder in King's Lynn who was so impressed at the child's perfect pitch, that he pointed it out to the Archbishop of Canterbury.

The party's first assault upon London was made when William was three-and-a-half, around New Year 1779. They stayed for the first week at the house of Sir Harbord Harbord, Bart., in Albemarle Street, after which they moved to lodgings in Piccadilly.

According to a letter from a Mr King (an artist who died young of a brain fever caused by drinking too much green tea), the infant

Crotch was introduced to Lady Dartmouth and John Christian Bach (son of J. S. Bach, and music master to the Queen). The latter arranged for William and his mother to visit Buckingham House, just as, a few years earlier, he had organised a similar excursion for the young Mozart.

Here they met the Prince Regent (later George IV), the Duke of Clarence (later William IV) and the reigning monarch, George III, who watched the small, dark-haired boy, perched on his mother's knee, playing a recital of short pieces entirely from memory. They were:

1. *God save great George our King*
2. *The bonny lad*
3. *The lad with the trowsers*
4. *The Graces*
5. *Gramachree Molly*
   (accompanied on the violin
   by the director of the King's
   Band, Wilhelm Cramer)
6. *Shepherds, I have lost my love*
7. *Bach's new March*
8. *The Thema*
9. *The Easter Hymn*
10. *An extempore voluntary*

On hearing *Gramachree Molly*, the King decided to test the child's ability to transpose. He therefore directed Cramer (who was accompanying on the violin) several times to change key. Each time Crotch followed, until he heard the Royal Command to return to the original key. The precocious infant turned round sharply to the King, and exclaimed "Why, don't be so silly"; at which the King roared with laughter, took the child in his arms, and ordered him a large tea!

Perhaps it was fortunate that John had not told his young brother that it *was* the King, since William had promised a maid-servant in Cambridge to convey a message from her whenever he should have the opportunity. This had already caused embarrass-ment to a gentleman who had wanted William to perform when he was out of humour. Mrs Crotch, to encourage him, had whispered, "Billy, it's the King"; at which William, remembering his promise, had blurted out, "King, Molly sends you her love!"

It was not only tact which the small boy lacked. Dr Burney was disappointed to find that his musical taste was quite undiscriminating. "I examined his countenance when he first heard the voice of Signor Pacchierotti, the principal singer of the Opera, but did not find that he seemed sensible of the superior taste and refinement of that exquisite performer; however, he called out very soon after the air was begun, 'He is singing in F'." A middle-aged Crotch later reflected that it was hardly surprising that he had not appreciated the stylised singing of an Italian, especially as he sang consistently flat.

Although the infant Crotch was famous for his musical precocity, he also showed potential as an artist. Before he was three, his drawings were attracting attention, and indeed, he would spend much time on the floor with a piece of chalk, often refusing to leave it to demonstrate on the organ. His childhood sketches of violins, windmills and ships provided him with an escape from the unnatural upheavals of travelling from town to town, and from the pressures of being a public spectacle every hour of the day.

His brother John was the only person who allowed young William to behave like other children of his age. He built him a model ship, taught him the complexities of its rigging and had naval battles with him. And he would take the boy to see the military parades which he so enjoyed watching. On one of these occasions, seeing that a soldier's feet were not properly turned out, William ran out and adjusted them to the right angle.

In 1779, although the child was still only four, Dr Burney announced that it was time for him to be given lessons. On the other hand, there were difficulties, the chief of which was William's arrogance and his unwillingness to learn. Of course, he could be forced to learn, but such a process might permanently destroy the spontaneity of his performance. In any case, Mrs Crotch was in financial difficulties, having spent more than she should on lodgings, and the extra expense of formal tuition had therefore to be ruled out.

William continued to be billed as "the self-taught musical child".

CHAPTER TWO

The Child

THE sweetmeats used by audiences to bribe young Crotch to perform may well have been the cause of a dangerous worm-fever which he contracted in March 1779. Certainly this was Mrs Crotch's opinion, since she took to dipping his sweetmeats in 'basket salt', with the result that he would no longer touch them when they were offered. These measures, however, failed to prevent another attack of the fever in May.

During this illness John, who had returned to Norwich to live with his father for a few months, arrived back in London to join William and his mother. Soon all three were on the move again.

In Oxford, the four-year-old met the Professor of Music, Dr Hayes, who doubtless had no inkling that he was talking to his successor. There then followed visits to Ware, Cambridge, Ely, Norwich, Thetford, Bury St Edmunds and Sudbury, with a return to London in mid-October. Here the child was taken by John Stanley, the blind organist of the Temple Church and Master of the King's Band, to hear Handel's oratorios; and he met for the first time the two brothers who had both been infant prodigies before him, Charles and Samuel Wesley (now aged twenty-two and nearly fourteen). A lifelong friendship developed between the latter and William.

With John's help, William had recently taught himself to play the violin, which he held as though it was a 'cello, and bowed with his left hand. On his first meeting with Samuel Wesley, the older boy tested his ear by purposely mistuning William's instrument. This invariably brought on the rage of the little boy, who would tell him whether it was tuned too high or too low. He also proved that he could distinguish between the mean-tone and the natural scales, and that his perfect pitch was therefore accurate to the nearest quarter-tone.

Furthermore, he showed that he could transpose from a major key into a minor, as well as into such unusual keys as F sharp minor.

The first of these accomplishments was proved with some difficulty, since when Master Wesley played a short piece in the minor mode a few times, little Crotch happened to be out of humour. Knowing that the child would sometimes play from pique when pleading had had no effect, Samuel played the treble only, and told William that he was far too young to be able to add the bass part to it. At this, he sat down by Samuel and accompanied him with the correct bass, first in the minor, then in the major.

The following years saw William, his mother and John engaged in an almost-unbroken tour, which took them to Worcester, Birmingham, Lichfield, Manchester, Chester, Liverpool, Sheffield, Wakefield, Halifax, York, Ripon, Durham, Newcastle-upon-Tyne and Edinburgh (1780); Perth, Dundee, Ayr, Montrose, Aberdeen Carlisle, Penrith, Kendal, Dumfries, Glasgow and many other musical centres (1781).

Till the age of nine, in fact, Crotch led the life of a traveller. No sooner was he reconciled to a new home, no sooner did he find a new playmate, than he would be whisked off to the next town. His own account of that time, written in his fifties, is frank and to-the-point:

"I look back on this part of my life with pain and humiliation . . . the manner in which my uncultivated abilities had been displayed to audiences who were frequently as ignorant of what was good and correct as myself and bestowed on me the most extravagant praises and dangerous flatteries, the attentions I received from ye great, the noble and the fair, . . . and the consciousness of possessing a musical ear such as everybody had not, made me think myself a most consequential being. I said the rudest things I could invent, being sure I should hear them repeated as good jokes; I was indulged in all my wishes as far as it was practicable; I was becoming a spoilt child and in danger of becoming what too many of my musical brethren have become under similar circumstances and unfortunately remained thro' life. Every young lady was called my future wife, and tho' I was too young to be introduced to Master Cupid, I had eyes enough to see his Mama; and whenever the prettiest lady in company was not standing by me, I would push the inferior beauty away from me. 'I don't like you; you are not pretty. *You* come here and stand by me; you are very pretty'."

The only instruction William received during these years came from his brother John, who taught him the names of the notes and the basis of reading and writing. John taught music in the reverse of the normal way, by placing before his brother the score of a piece which he had already learned from memory, and William responded quickly to this unconventional method. His reading was reasonably good by the age of five, and though he had a particularly good memory for whole words, he had a great aversion to spelling and spelling-books.

In a letter William wrote to his father in January 1783 (when he was seven-and-a-half) his hand appears still to have been guided, but soon afterwards he was writing by himself, as easily with his right hand as with his left. In fact, he once demonstrated this ability by writing, first with his right hand, then with his left, and finally backwards with his left hand—a trick he learned in 1788, when he cut the thumb of his right hand:

Throughout his life, Crotch drew and painted with his left hand, which he also used for bowing the violin and the 'cello, and for shooting with a bow and arrow (a hobby when he was young).

In July 1781, Mrs Crotch decided that her six-year-old son needed a change of image. He abandoned the "frocks" which he had worn until then, and which look so enchanting in engravings of him as an infant, and donned in their place a scarlet jacket and "trowsers".

That was the signal for more grand tours. In later life, Crotch would always connect certain towns with incidents which he remembered from this time. For example, at Chester he witnessed a fatal accident on the race course, at which his brother John fetched a plank to carry away the corpse; the same evening an actor expired on stage as he sat in the theatre.

In York, a patron, Dr Hunter, gave William a silver medal which for some years he would wear round his neck. In Edinburgh, John made some highly successful indoor fireworks to amuse his young brother, and the two of them spent much time walking and climbing the surrounding hills. In the same city, a blind philosopher, Dr Blacklock, gave William a flageolet on which he liked to perform in public. Then at Aberdeen, John was taught the art of tuning—a skill which he used later, when he became a musical instrument tuner and repairer in London.

In Carlisle, the future Conductor of the Concert of Ancient Music and Organist of Westminster Abbey, Thomas Greatorex, wrote down a minuet and some variations on *God save great George our King,* which William had composed at the keyboard; and in Hull, Crotch first learned to dance, and acquired a liking for jigsaw puzzles. A violin-maker in Nottingham gave him a fiddle whose strings were tuned back-to-front, to enable him to play left-handed and in a more conventional position; and here also William became acquainted with the organist Pearson, an excellent player who possessed only seven fingers.

The six-year-old was still as curt in his language as the four-year-old had been. One day in Glasgow, he was drawing on the floor when a lady played a note on the harpsichord and asked him to name it without looking. William said it was A-sharp, and to everybody's surprise she told him he was wrong. She played the note again and received the same reply. After a third similar attempt, William jumped up and exclaimed, "Why, what is it then, pray?" "B-flat," she said; to which Crotch cried triumphantly, "What, are you so stupid as not to know that B-flat and A-sharp are the same thing?" The lady left, remarking on the way out that she trusted she never would forget.

In July 1781, Mrs Crotch received a letter from Mrs Cooke (wife of Benjamin Cooke, Organist of Westminster Abbey), enclosing a cutting from the Deaths column of the *Gentleman's Magazine,* which read: "The musical world have sustained a considerable loss in the death of Master Crotch, the Norwich infant, whose extempore performances on the organ so much astonished the world during the last two years."

But although this announcement may have been a little premature, it no doubt resulted from reports of one of William's frequent illnesses and accidents which were all too real.

He was unable to leave Derby in February 1783, after being wounded in the thigh by a bayonet from a little toy gun which fell from the top of his bed as he was sitting on it to undress. This was followed by measles, which at least had the advantage that it allowed him a rest from continual travelling and performing, and gave him a chance for some quiet drawing and reading.

But he was soon back in circulation, playing with amateur musicians in Ashby de la Zouch. Apparently the standard was not high—it was discovered at the end of one particular piece that a certain Dr Kirkland, an oboist, had been playing a different piece from the rest of the orchestra. On another occasion, William flew into a rage during a performance of an Abel overture which he was directing from the keyboard, when the horn players put down their instruments in order better to hear his playing.

At Northampton, an aged black dog called Julia was added to the party and caused great amusement with her grunts and groans which strongly resembled talking. William told one unfortunate lady who wished to hear him play: "Julia says, if you don't go away and stop bothering me, she'll eat you." "And who may Julia be?" she asked. At that moment, in walked the dog, growling, and although she had no teeth and could only hobble, the lady was taking no chances. She left hurriedly.

Throughout their journeyings, William had been supported by a series of patrons, who would organise his stay in a particular town or city, promote concerts, introduce him to local musicians and celebrities, and sometimes provide financial assistance. One of the most important in his early years had been Dr Burney. Sir George Saville, too, had not only helped in every possible way, but used to enjoy entertaining William with drawings and strange mechanical devices which he had built. On a visit to Oxford during the summer of 1783, Crotch first met another benefactor who was to prove important to him, the Reverend Alexander Goucher Schomberg.

At first when friends suggested a visit to see William, Schomberg could see no reason why he should put himself out, in order to hear an eight-year-old "jingle the keys of a harpsichord and scrape imperfect tones from the strings of a diminutive fiddle". But after some weeks he relented, and went round to the Crotches' lodgings with a couple of friends.

They arrived, the last of a number of parties, long after the proper bedtime for a boy of William's age. He was sitting at a harpsichord on his mother's knee, dressed in a yellow-and-white striped linen jacket and trousers.

He played two pieces, stopping during the first to name the notes of a peal of bells which started up outside. After the second, Schomberg asked Mrs Crotch to close the harpsichord so that he could put some questions to her, while William squatted in a corner reading a book.

When Schomberg had heard the story which Mrs Crotch told to visitors at least a dozen times every day, he turned to William and asked him to read aloud from his book. "Oh sir," he said eagerly, "I can read something better than this." He brought out a farce called *Too civil by half,* which a gentleman had left an hour before, and he and Schomberg read a couple of scenes together, the boy entering into his rôles with great gusto. Possibly he had actually seen this acted on stage, since James Hook had composed the music for it only the previous year and it had received a number of performances in London.

At the same interview, William showed considerable excitement at the prospect of a puppet theatre which John had promised to build, with characters from William's favourite story, *Robinson Crusoe.* William was to write the music, and when Schomberg expressed surprise that he could compose, William replied by opening the harpsichord and playing a Sonata of his own—all the while talking to one of Schomberg's friends who was standing by the keyboard, and never once looking down at the keys.

As Schomberg left the room, he alluded to the farce by saying, "Good night, Aunt Bridget," to which William replied, with a formal curtsy, "Good night, sweet Uncle Toby." On the way home, Schomberg and his companions agreed that the boy was "a very uninteresting little fellow, not worth two straws of a foot long," and they resolved not to lift a finger to help him. However, they had agreed to entertain him to breakfast in Magdalen College the following morning, when perhaps he would give a different impression.

At breakfast, he apparently took greater pleasure in feeding the deer out of the window than in eating his own meal or talking to his hosts. Afterwards, strolling outside, he complained of a pain in his thigh.

In a conversation about his drawings of ships, William commented that it was a pity one could not paint the noise of the guns, as well as the smoke. Schomberg replied that painters and musicians each had their own jobs to do, and that the former could no more paint the report of a gun, than the latter could imitate smoke on the harpsichord. "Ah, well now you shall have them both together", announced Crotch, leading the way indoors and over to a harpsichord. He placed the picture which had sparked off the conversation—of a ship in the midst of battle—on the music stand and, thumping and rumbling out a formidable cannonade of bass notes with his knuckles, called out "Well done, my brave lads," "We'll make them strike," "Now a broadside!"

One evening, Crotch was sitting in the audience in the Oxford Music Room, when he was spotted by the leader of the band. "Will you play for us between the acts?" he asked. Mrs Crotch said he had no music with him, but the leader went over to a cupboard and picked up the first score that came to hand. "How about this piece of Clementi?" When the time came, Crotch sat down quietly at the keyboard and played it through. On such an occasion, he was already a responsible musician, by example rather than by any training. He would still play the part of the temperamental infant prodigy at home, but knew what was required of him by professional musicians.

However, his table manners still needed to be improved. Schomberg reported that at one meal William refused to eat the veal or roast pork or pie, and that he insisted on being served with mutton. When that came, he would not swallow more than a spoonful, but after turning it round and round, and over and over, dined at last upon two potatoes. Schomberg's comment afterwards: "A wayward trick such as we see in what are called spoiled children and might offend some folks." Then when William took his wine, he behaved "not respectfully, but rudely, nodding and winking round the table".

When, at the end of the meal, he was asked to sing, he said that he did not like singing, and that he had, in any case, never heard anybody sing perfectly in tune. In middle age, Crotch qualified this remark by asserting that he had heard singing that was more like perfection, and which reached nearer to the soul, than even the most exquisite instrumental sound; but to think "that persons who stand up for ye perfection of the voice should sit in raptures while some great Italian singer goes thro' a whole scene *half-a-note too flat,* moves my wonder."

William was due to arrive back from Reading on 21st July, 1783, to give a concert in Oxford the following day, but the hours passed, and there was no sign of his party. Finally at ten o'clock in the evening, John appeared, covered in mud, breathless and with his clothes torn. He stammered out the news that, eight miles outside Reading, at Basildon, their carriage had overturned, and both Mrs Crotch and William had been badly hurt. They were shortly brought in and taken to their beds.

It quickly became obvious that the injuries were not as bad as they might at first have seemed, but William had hurt his shoulder, and because of the pain it was causing, he had to abandon the original intention of leading the band the next day.

Nevertheless he insisted on appearing at the concert to play an organ concerto, a duet and a solo item. He seemed to be in some pain during the duet, after Dr Hayes had lifted him up onto the stool by the injured arm, but he continued to play. Afterwards a surgeon was called. He discovered that the collar bone was broken, and he bandaged it up tightly, with the words: "Well, little laddie, I hope you'll never be so brave again. I cannot imagine why you went on playing when you must have been in agony." Certainly there cannot be many musicians whose professionalism led them through a whole concert with a broken collar bone!

The surgeon was so impressed that he refused to take money for the six weeks of attention which followed. Instead he asked William to write him a piece of music as payment.

Schomberg was at last completely won over by the boy. He wrote that he had provided him in his old age with "as great a musical treat as I ever felt, and yet I remember the days of Handel . . . I sat at his elbow while he played and actually wept." He followed this with a fascinating comparison: "I heard both Charles and Samuel Wesley when they were a year or so older than Crotch, with not half the satisfaction. There is something so artless and wild both in his manners and his music, that it is impossible not to be captivated, whereas I always thought that the abovementioned had in both these articles too studied, too mechanical a manner."

But captivating or not, Crotch had reached the stage at which he could remain "self-taught" no longer. His musical performance had to be disciplined and directed along pre-ordained paths, and he must be given some form of general education. Schomberg saw that he had a lively curiosity and a high level of intelligence, and decided that now was therefore the time for him to make a start on Latin and Greek, which other boys of his age had already begun. Schomberg warned him that he must prepare for the day when he would put away childish things; the day when a liking for "boisterous basses and tumultuous harmonies" would be replaced by a taste for "affecting Adagios and tender Sicilianas"; when the "pictures of ancient Masters and noble remains of Greek and Roman Art" would be preferred to "views of naval actions and paste-board puppet shows in deal boxes". Schomberg wanted to introduce Crotch to Milton, Virgil and Shakespeare, where before he had known only *Robinson Crusoe* and *Too civil by half.*

He pressed home the point: "Unless it be your highest ambition to become an organist in a country town, to teach ladies at 30 shillings a quarter . . . riding a hackhorse round the neighbourhood with a profitable engagement at two genteel boarding schools . . . something else must be learnt besides the gamut and the finger-board."

Schomberg was, in any case, keen to end the unhealthy life which William had been leading. He told him that he was "a delicate little animal of no more bodily substance than an October hare", and that dancing was "too violent an exercise for such a wire-drawn carcase."

He pointed out the truth which Mrs Crotch refused to face: "Public curiosity is soon satisfied, and whatever Burgess or Cowper or Cabanel or myself may think of the matter will not be attracted much longer to your harpsichord or violin." Crotch himself looked back to those years and reflected: "My spirit was in a measure humbled, and by the time I was nine years old, I was timid, quiet, nervous, and altogether different from boys of ye same age."

Schomberg's first remedy was to advise early rising and early retiring, the avoidance of hot rooms, and prayer to God. After that came the problem of what form William's education should take.

CHAPTER THREE

Cambridge

MRS BURNEY gave William some lessons in French, and Schomberg succeeded in improving his table-manners, but the decision about his future still had to be made.

Daines Barrington suggested that he might be apprenticed to Samuel Wesley, but Schomberg was determined that the boy should become "a scholar and a gentleman", like Dr Burney—or William Jackson of Exeter, or Charles Avison (late organist of Newcastle-upon-Tyne) or Rameau (the composer)— all of whom were respected and welcomed wherever they went; he pointed out that more ignorant orchestral musicians could never be received in genteel company.

An offer was made of a place at Rugby School, but Schomberg realised that a delicate boy of Crotch's temperament and background would have been bullied relentlessly by the other boys. In any case, he knew no Latin whatsoever, and would therefore have found it difficult to keep up with his contemporaries.

Another possibility was that William should become a chorister either at the Chapel Royal or at Magdalen College, Oxford. Schomberg, however, thought that he should "nurse that thin small voice" for the time being.

In the event, after a few months at home in Norwich, Crotch took up residence with his mother in Cambridge (in April 1786), as Assistant to the Professor of Music, Dr Randall. First, though, he finished composing the music to a farce called *Transformation, or Spanish Philosophy,* for performance at the Norwich Theatre; and his arrival in Cambridge coincided with the appearance of his first published musical composition, *Dear liberty, grant me a smile,* a song for solo voice and keyboard accompaniment (the latter containing some rather awkward turns of phrase which seem to make the pianist's or harpsichordist's task unnecessarily difficult). And soon afterwards he composed two sonatas.

William and his mother settled in lodgings in Shoemaker Row (now Market Street), and although he was not himself a member of the University, he was taught by men who were. He was instructed in Latin, in turn, by Tindal Thompson Walmsley (a graduate of St John's College who had been at school and college with William Wilberforce), Mr Owen (of Bene't—now Corpus Christi—College), a personal friend of Schomberg, and William Johnson (an undergraduate of St John's and six years William's senior), while his study of Italian was directed by Signor Isola (of Sidney Sussex College). Crotch once admitted: "What a provoking brat I must have been. I could learn nothing, I could teach myself anything. Latin was hateful to me, Italian rather irksome when taught"—a condemnation, might one suggest, more of the teaching methods employed than of Crotch?

More important in his own eyes were his musical duties which, after a benefit concert in King's College Hall in May 1786, settled down into a regular routine of daily services. These culminated each week in an exhausting Sunday programme, when William would play the organ for six services—two in King's College Chapel, two in Trinity, two in Great St Mary's (the University Church) and occasionally a seventh in St John's when the organist, Jonathan Sharpe, was away.

As the Professor grew more and more infirm, he entrusted more of the playing to young Crotch, who was thus forced to acquire fluency in the skills of a Cathedral organist—reading and transposing at sight, and improvising in a "church style". Indeed, he could easily have earned his living in the cathedral organ loft.

Not all his time was spent in Cambridge, however, for William and his mother were in London for the 1786 Handel celebrations in Westminster Abbey. One of the boy's patrons, James Crane, took him to see a number of operas, and he spent much of his time in the metropolis with an old friend from Norwich, Charles Hague. Then at a performance of Handel's *Messiah* in the Abbey, William was befriended by one of the altos in the chorus, who sat him in the orchestra for the concert.

Back in Cambridge, Crotch played the drums at the Commencement Service, and was responsible for keeping the orchestra from hurrying in the chorus *Sing unto God* (from Handel's *Judas Maccabæus*), when no amount of shouting or hand-clapping from the conductor, Dr Randall, had had the slightest effect. He always treasured the Professor's quiet words after the service: "Good boy."

Handel was at this period still the dominant influence on English music, and Crotch became well-versed in his music through the efforts of Professor Randall, who had known the great man. Apparently Handel had always called the Professor "Queen Esther", a part he remembered him singing as a chorister in the oratorio *Esther*. An Undergraduate news sheet of about 1778 referred to the fact in a piece of doggerel:

> "Queen Esther was sung by young Randall,
> By the light of a solitary candle;
> But when nicknamed 'Queen Esther' by Handel,
> Then we all thought it rather a scandal."

William frequently presided (that is, directed the orchestra from the harpsichord) at the Cambridge Concerts at Petty Cury which, quite apart from anything else, taught him the arts of orchestral score-reading and thorough-bass realisation. He would also join with his friend Charles Hague, who was now studying in Cambridge, to give fortnightly performances in the 'Black Bear'. Hague, who had studied the violin with Salomon, would lead a small orchestra and sing, while William would play Handel organ concertos and Clementi harpsichord sonatas.

William was introduced to whole areas of the musical repertory with which most musicians would have been unfamiliar, at weekly musical evenings. They were held at the homes of Dr Jowett (Under Master of Trinity Hall) and Dr Hey (of Sidney Sussex College), and it was here that he heard music from all over Europe, including "ancient music" (roughly speaking, music more than a century old), which was to form his taste and judgement for the future.

Although he lived with his mother, William must have seemed a lonely figure in University life. At any rate, there was no lack of sympathy and help. He was befriended by Dr Hinchcliffe (Bishop of Peterborough and Master of Trinity) and welcomed by his wife and family. Similar attentions were lavished on him by Dr Peckhard (Dean of Carlisle), Dr Breadon (Master of Jesus College and later vice Chancellor of the University) and Fellows of Caius, Queens', Magdalene, King's and Trinity. An undergraduate, Mr Willins of Caius, helped him with his Latin, and he became friendly with undergraduates from Trinity; Emmanuel and St John's.

In September 1786, Schomberg sent William an oratorio text, *Captivity of Judah,* which he once set to music, dedicating the work to Schomberg and his friend Owen. It was his first attempt at large-scale composition, and he was aided by Charles Hague, and by the latter's own teacher, the Dutch composer who had for many years lived in Cambridge, Pieter Helendaal, who corrected and revised the final version. Some years later, Crotch was shown a criticism of the work by the Reverend Thomas Twining (of Colchester), who, while agreeing that it was an extraordinary product by an eleven-year-old, said that it was nevertheless "all the work of *ear,* recollection and *âtonnement,* without regular musical training"; he pointed to "gross faults and slovenliness of harmony", and was not able to find any "passages of melody that are not old and trite and dry", though "many of the choruses are well designed", and the composer had "a good idea of grand choral effect and expression". He recommended the study of harmony and of the music of the Italian opera composers which Crotch despised.

Crotch later agreed, "I was not yet (at 11 years of age) capable of writing a correct harmony or of making a correct answer to a subject", and as a sign of respect to Schomberg, he wrote an entirely new setting to the same libretto when he was at his peak as a composer.

More successful than this early oratorio were two songs, the first a setting of words by Cowper, *A rose had been washed,* the other, *Sycamore Vale,* with a text by Miss Garland of Norwich (probably a relation of the organist of the cathedral).

In his spare time in Cambridge, Crotch continued to pursue his many non-musical interests—drawing, balloons and fireworks among them. He corresponded with his brother John (now living in Norwich) on the subject of fortifications, and became, with the help of a book called *The Field of Mars,* so expert in the subject that Schomberg concluded that he would end in mathematics or madness. Not content with that, William acquired a pair of globes and became fascinated by both geography and astronomy.

During his two years in Cambridge, Crotch underwent a transformation. In June 1787, he said farewell to his jacket and "trowsers", which were replaced by short "kneed breeches" and long skirted coats—a change which he did not welcome, since it exposed a malformation of his knees, which he had inherited from his father, and for which in 1788 a surgeon prescribed cold bathing. His friends, however, preferred the new look, Hague being heard to comment: "A friend in kneed, is a friend indeed".

Schomberg found William greatly improved in his "general manner and deportment", and both he and Dr Jowett favoured another move for the boy—this time to Oxford to read for the Church. Serious doubts about the wisdom of this decision were expressed by Mrs Crotch, as well as by Dr Cooke (of Westminster Abbey) and William Jackson (of Exeter), who thought that a more general education, with specialisation in music, would be more useful.

While plans were being discussed, William and his mother returned briefly to Norwich, where family tempers flared (for some time Mrs Crotch's financial difficulties had been the cause of contention between her and her husband, and indeed, it was rarely that the two of them now met at all), and as if to announce William's new life and the final dispersal of the family, there was a violent thunderstorm, and a nearby house was struck by lightning.

William was so perturbed that, on returning to Cambridge and seeing Schomberg, he became so excited that he completely forgot to play the last psalm during a service in King's Chapel. Then, walking out of the College and across King's Parade to Bene't (Corpus Christi) College—which he did every day—he became hopelessly lost and had to ask his way.

In May 1788, Mrs Crotch reluctantly agreed to allow William to go to Oxford. She herself refused to return to her husband in Norwich, and decided to remain in Cambridge, making William promise to pay her a visit once a year.

On the way to Oxford, Crotch passed through London and attended the trial of Warren Hastings, where he heard Charles Fox speak, and saw Lord North slumped in his seat fast asleep.

CHAPTER FOUR

Oxford

DURING his two years in Cambridge, William had learned the fundamental skills of a cathedral musician. He had been introduced to large areas of the orchestral repertory, and he had gleaned at least an elementary knowledge of the Classics and of English literature. In Oxford he was expected to build on this training.

He arrived in June 1788, and went to lodge with Mr Matthews, a Yeoman Beadle who kept a music shop in the High Street. Matthews was a bass in the Christ Church Cathedral choir, and he at once showed his support for William by making a fair copy of his oratorio *Captivity of Judah*. The rest of the family comprised Mrs Matthews, two daughters (one living at home, the other married) and a son, William, a Demy of Magdalen College, who became Crotch's Latin tutor. A teacher with a pigtail called Monsieur de la Salle also lodged in the house, and he gave William lessons in French.

William Matthews was a fine 'cellist and harpsichordist, and he and Crotch spent much time making music together. They also pursued a mutual interest in producing puppet shows.

For the first of these shows, *Ye grand ballet of Cupid and Psyche,* Crotch painted the scenery and compiled the music (which included many well-known tunes). Then at the performances, which took place in Matthews's rooms in Magdalen, the two Williams controlled the dolls, whilst highly dramatic thunder-effects were manufactured in the room above.

Their next production was *Il Cavaliero Bertrando (or Il trionfo d'Amore),* this time with scenery by the painter Roberts, and music composed and selected by Crotch. This time, Crotch was presiding at the harpsichord, though his place was infrequently taken by William Matthews, and on one occasion by Charles Wesley. They had a small orchestra, and although the show was not open to the public, friends and patrons provided loyal support; even the Duke and Duchess of Marlborough appeared for one performance.

During his first year in Oxford, Crotch was able to devote his time more than ever before to such hobbies as riding his new grey pony, which he called Christopher, and experimenting, together with his friend Robert Bliss, with the mysteries of electricity (which resulted in at least one nasty shock).

In June 1789, on the first of William's annual visits to see his mother in Cambridge, part of his oratorio *Captivity of Judah* was performed in the Hall of Trinity Hall, to an audience which included Prince William of Gloucester and Dr Jowett. But sad news reached him in Oxford only months later; his patron Schomberg had failed to be elected to the coveted Professorship of Civil Law in Cambridge, and early in 1790, he had caught a "rheumatic fever" after being twice soaked to the skin. He lost the use of his legs, and had little choice but to reduce his financial support to Crotch, who had to dispose of both his pony and a sitting-room which he had been using a few doors down the street from his lodgings.

Almost on his death-bed, the old man finally realised that it would be useless to continue in his campaign to make a scholar of Crotch. He bowed to the undeniable truth, admitting that his protégé must be allowed to pursue the profession of music unhindered. He must be allowed to become the "compleat musician", rather than a "compleat gentleman".

Schomberg did not actually die until March 1792, but the way was now open for William to follow the trade to which he had been born. Indeed, his gratitude to Schomberg for this change of mind— and for all his previous help—was made clear many years later, when Crotch referred to him as "the dearest friend I ever had".

In September 1789, when William was fourteen, Thomas Norris, the Organist of Christ Church, died and Crotch's patrons lost no time in recommending him to the Dean, Dr Cyril Jackson. He was at once appointed to the post of Cathedral Organist, a position which rendered him and his mother financially self-sufficient at last. No longer did they have to rely on the generosity of friends and patrons.

With the job there went a small hut with a fireplace and two windows, surrounded by a garden, and it was here that the choristers rehearsed. Crotch found some furniture and a harpsichord, and inaugurated a series of small concerts there.

At about this time, he suddenly woke up in the middle of one night after he had dreamt the final sixteen bars of a piece of music. He at once wrote them down, and used them as the ending for the music to a play based on a subject from Virgil. Unfortunately, though, he never completed the score.

In the summer of 1791, William was in London to hear one of Salomon's concerts in which Haydn was directing one of his own symphonies from the piano. As was the custom at this period, the audience applauded every movement, and actually encored both the *Andante* and the *Finale*. Soon afterwards Haydn visited Oxford to have an honorary doctorate conferred on him, and when Salomon took him into Christ Church Cathedral, Crotch performed a short organ recital in his honour, including a chorus from Handel's *Israel in Egypt, The Lord shall reign*. Later, over dinner, William played to him, this time on the harpsichord, the programme consisting of a sonata by Samuel Wesley and an overture of Crotch's own composition.

Crotch matriculated at St Mary's Hall (which allowed him to proceed to his degree), and began to build a piano-teaching practice which included a number of pupils from among the local nobility. His activities were interrupted, however, by a final journey to see his patron Schomberg, now in Bath and a very sick man. On the way, he heard Haydn directing selections from operas at the Opera House in London, and when he arrived in Bath, he read a book which was to influence his own theoretical writings, and indeed, on which he was to base much of his teaching, Sir Joshua Reynolds's *Lectures on Painting*.

The previous October (1790), William Matthews had left Oxford to become a curate, and on 4th December, 1791, his father died, leaving Crotch homeless. He had a choice either to move into the house of a Mr Slatten, who had taught him arithmetic, or to join the Bliss family, of whom his "electrically-minded" friend Robert Bliss was a member. He decided on the latter.

Mr Bliss, a bookseller in the High Street, and, like the late Mr Matthews, a Yeoman Beadle, was the son of the late Professor of Astronomy at Oxford (and afterwards Astronomer Royal at Greenwich), and an inherited interest in the subject was passed on to Crotch. Even more compelling a preoccupation however came to be centred on Mr Bliss's daughter, Martha, who was a year younger than William, and whom he eventually married. Crotch sentimentalised in his bed-ridden fifties: "The early choice of a partner for life is the next blessing to Religion itself. My Martha was . . . [in] every way suited to my wishes."

William seems to have been a well-known figure in Oxford even at this time. A description, probably by John Skinner of Trinity College, of a day spent in College in the winter of 1792, shows that his famous childhood commanded both joking and respect:

> "Warren and self in gloomy weather
> Ofttimes a number get together
> Immediately we dine,
> Who sit and chat till half-past five
> With jest and song are all alive
> With quite sufficient wine.
>
> Then Crotch and two musicians more
> And amateurs near half a score
> To play in concert meet.
> Our chairs to Warren's rooms we move
> And those who strains melodious love
> Enjoy a real treat.
>
> Crotch, as director of the band,
> On harpsichord with rapid hand
> Sweeps the full chord:— this youth
> Of late thro' Britain's realms was styl'd
> The wondrous boy—Apollo's child—
> And such he was in truth.
>
> For when five summers he had told
> And scarce his hands a bow could hold
> He Handel's pieces knew;
> The time and harmony would note
> Not like a parrot, all by rote,
> But as a Master true.
>
> Whilst years increas'd and science more
> Augmented still his copious store,
> His genius brighter shone;
> By pencil prov'd and just design
> Such knowledge in the graphic line
> As very few have done.

In such a lib'ral age as this
And such a place where merit is
Or ought to be repaid,
May then his highly gifted mind
Some fost'ring friends and Patron find
And thrive in Oxford's shade."

Crotch took up two new hobbies, skating and fencing, but they proved too violent, since he had more knee trouble—it was said that his left knee-pan had been "put out". In any case, he was forced to wear a bandage for some months to prevent a recurrence. The weakness continued, however, so that thirty years later he was complaining of very weak knees, and after that his ankles, too, caused trouble.

It is refreshing to see that William's fertile imagination, as expressed in drawings and puppet-shows, was still active in non-musical spheres. A charming brief autobiography, written when he was about sixteen, perhaps makes the present biography super-fluous!:

"William Crotch. Born at Norwich, on the 5th of July 1775 in Greens-Lane St George's Colgate, Norfolk, England, Europe, World. —W. Crotch chang'd his name to James Wright, and was shipwrecked on an uninhabited island; on his being released he came to England—was made a gentleman—presently a Lord—then a Duke—then an English King—then a King of England—then King of Britain—and then a King of the World—and then changed back his name to his former one, viz.: W.C.—a fairy gave him as much power as herself—He therefore conjured all the old people into Giants from 12 to 1 mile high—then lived happy—part in the Island of Guai, and part in Britain—seldom out of these places—King Pepin & George III his friend.

Wm. Crotch, Mr Bliss' Bookseller, High St St Mary's Parish, Oxford—Oxfordshire—England—Great Britain, Europe, Terra, Solar System, one of a cluster in the milky way, one of the Stratas."

In 1793, Crotch published three pianoforte sonatas by sub-scription, and was greatly encouraged by the approval of the leader of the Oxford Music Room orchestra, Johann Baptist Malchair.

On 5th June 1794, William took his degree of Bachelor in Music. The examiner, Dr Hayes, remarked that the submitted composition seemed to include a section taken from another work, and indeed he was quite right. A former production had in fact been inserted by Crotch—one which the Professor had never seen or heard. Despite this, the composition was accepted, and received performances both at the Music School and at the Music Room.

The work highlights the position of the clarinet at this period, since it was by no means accepted as an instrument to be included in the orchestral ensemble. It was used as a solo instrument, and for this particular work, John Mahon, who was leading the band, himself played the clarinet obbligato part in one of the arias.

In May, William Matthews had visited Oxford, and he and Crotch had gone riding together. Only six months later, Crotch received news that his friend was dead—the first of a long series of early deaths which made Crotch both lonely and resigned. About the same time, he was attacked by a succession of boils culminating in an abscess, whose opening by a surgeon seemed to result in a visible improvement in his physical health.

Crotch now decided that Oxford ought to have a Harmonic Society of composers like that which his friend Charles Hague had established in Cambridge. In August 1796, therefore, the Harmonic Society of Oxford came into being, with Crotch as President and a distinguished and highly-exclusive membership, which included Thomas Attwood (a former pupil of Mozart, who in that year—1796—was appointed Organist of St Paul's Cathedral), Dr Charles Burney, William Beale (later organist of Trinity College, Cambridge), William Horsley (an organist and composer of vocal music), John Callcott (a popular glee composer), Joseph Pring (organist of Bangor Cathedral), William Jackson (organist of Exeter Cathedral and a distinguished landscape painter), John Marsh (a wealthy amateur composer who wrote music with proficiency, built a quarter-tone harpsichord and made plans for converting the Jews to Anglican Christianity), and Cipriani Potter (a pupil of both Crotch and Callcott, and later Crotch's successor as Principal of the Royal Academy of Music). Not all these composers joined at the Society's inception, but those who did agreed that its aim should be "the encouragement and improvement of musical compositions"; and as a result of the efforts of its members, there survive three manuscript volumes of compositions which they wrote.

They include rounds, chansons, glees, canons, madrigals and "motetts". Crotch contributed 104 items, the first dated 24th

August 1796, the last dated 30th January 1823, though regular entries had ceased in 1803. Some of Crotch's more bizarre offerings include a "contrapunto" (an invention of Dr Burney, featuring among its contrapuntal intricacies both inversion and retro-inversion), an "Epitaph on the gravestone of Tallis" (set to the words: "Entomed here doth by a worthy wyght/Who for long tyme in musick bore/The bell his name to show was/Thomas Tallis . . ."), and a round in which the voices imitate the ringing of church-bells: "Bimbim, bembem, bambam. . .".

The Society never actually met, the book of compositions being loaned to each member in turn for a limited period. This avoided the difficulties which caused the collapse of the Cambridge Society—"the meeting in small parties of persons widely differing in rank, sentiment and principles from each other", as Crotch put it. Thus, no quarrels and equally, no official performances.

CHAPTER FIVE

Professor Crotch

OXFORD students at the end of the eighteenth century were not as appreciative of the finer points of music-making as perhaps they might have been. It was thus not uncommon for disturbances to occur at orchestral concerts in the Music Room, and on one occasion (in about 1792) during an audience riot, the valuable violin belonging to Malchair, the leader, was badly damaged by an orange thrown by a drunken student. Malchair, stunned by the loss of his priceless instrument, at once retired.

It was a sad occasion, since Malchair had been leader of the orchestra for more than thirty years, and was a highly respected figure in the University. For Crotch, too, it was a blow, since he and Malchair had become firm friends. The old man would visit the youth every day between four o'clock and ten-to-five, often bringing a new tune for Crotch's collection—the collection which was to form the basis for his three-volume *Specimens of Various Styles of Music*. They also shared an interest in a number of subjects, from water-colour painting to religion.

Soon after the incident with the violin, Dr Philip Hayes, the Professor, was so disgusted by remarks shouted at a friend and pupil of his in the orchestra, a Mr Webb, that he too resigned, and Crotch was asked to take over direction of the concerts. He directed from the harpsichord until 1805, usually choosing varied programmes of both vocal and instrumental items, and often including performances of Haydn's *Salomon* symphonies, at least one of which he could claim to have heard under the direction of the composer.

Dr Hayes died suddenly in London in March 1797, and early in April, the electors for the Professorship met to decide on his successor. They were the Vice-Chancellor and the heads of the choirs of Christ Church, New College, Magdalen and St John's, of whom two (the Dean of Christ Church and Dr Marlow of St John's)

39

were in fact Crotch's patrons. To add to this connection, the Vice-Chancellor was a close friend of the Dean of Christ Church, and these three, in putting forward Crotch's name, therefore had a majority. Dr Gauntlett (of New College) and Dr Routh (of Magdalen) were not, in any case, opposed to the appointment, even though the latter had intended to support another name, that of John Beckwith, the organist of Norwich Cathedral and sometime organist for Dr Hayes in Magdalen Chapel.

Crotch was thus elected unanimously to the Professorship, though he was still only twenty-one, and he retained the office for just over fifty years, until his death. Such an unlikely-sounding election is only partly explained by the patronage of certain of the electors. It must also be remembered that the appointment of young men to similar positions was not uncommon in the Academic world at this period, and indeed, the position of Prime Minister had, only fifteen years earlier, been taken by a man of the same age, the younger Pitt. In any case, apart from a casual mention of John Beckwith, there were no other candidates.

The death of Dr Hayes also left vacant the posts of organist at St John's College and at both the University Church and the Theatre. Crotch was appointed to all three. He took on two apprentices of the late Professor as assistants, and he became the owner of the Professor's garden behind the Holywell Music Room.

The contrast between the appearance of the late Professor and that of his replacement did not go unnoticed. The tall, bulky Professor Hayes and the short, slight Crotch were the subject of a piece of verse entitled *Trying it on:*

"At length when the big Doctor died
  (Weighed down by his fame and his fat),
His light-weighing successor tried
  To succeed to his gown and his hat.

But the three-cornered hat would not do,
  And the gown (if report you'll believe)
Was too large, even cut into two, —
  So they made him a gown of a sleeve."

Perhaps the crowning event in a year of achievement and good fortune was Crotch's marriage, on 10th July, to Martha Bliss, whose family he had been living with. His delightfully eighteenth-century description of their courtship tells how he had "admired her for nine, loved her for seven, and courted her for five years".

The couple moved into a house in Broad (Clarendon) Street, where Crotch built an observatory on the roof, from which he could further his study of the stars and planets and his researches and observations on thunderstorms. Before they settled in, though, they visited William's mother in Cambridge, calling at London both on the way and on the way back. They met a number of William's friends and patrons, and called on brother John, who had joined Broadwood's as a tuner in 1791, and was now setting up his own business.

On their return to Oxford, Crotch's wife Martha became almost addicted to exercise. She would walk four times round the Parks, three times round Christ Church Meadow and up Cumner Hill as a regular event. Unfortunately her husband was unable to do the same, since early in 1798 his right leg became inflamed, necessitating a short while in bed. Later the same year, he was complaining of a fever.

One of the duties of the Professor was the adjudication of musical compositions submitted as exercises for the degrees of Mus.Bac. and Mus.Doc. It therefore fell upon Professor Crotch to judge his own Mus.Doc. exercise in 1799. Hardly surprisingly it fulfilled the Professorial requirements, though to be fair, it is reasonably certain that it would have been accepted, whoever had been in the Chair.

The composition was a setting of Warton's *Ode to Fancy* (a text also set to music by two other members of Crotch's Harmonic Society, John Callcott and William Jackson), in this version scored for two four-part choruses, three soloists (S.T.B.) and a small symphony orchestra of strings, flutes, bassoons, horns, trumpet and timpani with harpsichord and organ continuo. The work contains some fine moments, not least of which is the firm and dramatic opening subject (for chorus basses, with bassoons and double basses in unison) of the fugue, *Who fill'd with unexhausted fire:*

FUGA - Allegro

Unison: Chor. basses, bassoons, bassi

Who fill'd with un - ex - hau - sted fire may bold-ly smite the sound-ing lyre, may bold-

In December 1798, the new Professor inaugurated a series of lectures, similar in style to their modern counterparts, but a departure from current practice. At first, he was assisted by the Music Room orchestra, after which he would himself demonstrate points at the piano. Audiences included distinguished members of the University (Masters of Colleges and Professors in other disciplines) as well as undergraduates. There was no music faculty in the modern sense; nor was there any formal course of musical instruction.

Crotch's lectures became a regular feature of Oxford life, and his articles were widely read—articles by no means restricted to musical scholarship. The *Monthly Magazine* of 1800 carried an explanation by Crotch of the shape of the earth and the atmosphere of the moon, as well as an article advocating the use of the pendulum as a metronome. From this date onwards, Crotch's compositions all bear tempi directions in terms of swings of the pendulum, and after about 1815 (the year in which Maelzel discovered Winkel's invention, the mechanical metronome and began to manufacture them himself), he would use both scales; thus a piece of music might be prefaced:

> Pendulum: one quaver equals 10 inch.
> Maelzel's Metronome: 126

or:

> Pendm.: one minim = 20 inch.
> M.M. = 88.

CHAPTER SIX

Crotch's Musical Teachings

CROTCH'S theories on music had considerable influence on a number of young composers and performers. Ninety years after the first lectures (and articles in the *Monthly Magazine,* which expounded the same ideas), Sir John Stainer blamed Crotch's teachings for the ruin of at least one promising composing career (he was referring to that of Sir Frederick Gore Ouseley). He pointed bitterly to what he called Crotch's "blind imitation of the past".

The pupils themselves, however, held their teacher in great respect. Sir George Elvey, Sir William Sterndale Bennett, Sir John Goss, Ouseley and Dr Corfe all joined in an attempt, unsuccessful as it happened, to secure the posthumous publication of Crotch's final oratorio, the second version of *Captivity of Judah.*

The only way to understand the true situation is to read the lectures, articles and theoretical works oneself, but a summary of their contents must here suffice.

Crotch, the musician and painter, believed in the interrelation of the arts, and adapted Sir Joshua Reynolds's theories of painting to music. Thus all music, regardless of age or nationality, could be classed within one or more of three basic categories; the sublime, the beautiful and the ornamental.

Only the highest, the most lofty and dignified music could be considered sublime. Therefore, just as Michaelangelo's works formed a highpoint of sublimity in painting, so Handel's choruses and Bach's organ fugues provided a similar peak in music. The "pure sublime" had, however, reached absolute perfection even earlier, with the "true church style" of the sixteenth and early seventeenth-century composers in Italy and England, Palestrina, Byrd and Gibbons. Music had been becoming less dignified ever since.

Truly pathetic, solemn, sublime music might be produced in a number of ways; as, for example, when a few simple notes are performed in octaves or in unison by voices or instruments; or when "the harmony is clear and simple, but the melody and measure dignified and marked", as in the first chorus of Handel's *Saul;* or when the harmony and modulations are "learned and mysterious", and the ear is in consequence unable to anticipate the next chord; or when large instrumental and choral forces combine in great grandeur.

The second category, the beautiful, was the result of softness, delicacy, gentle modulations, symmetry and sweetness, together with simple and intelligible harmony, as exemplified by Corelli's *Pastorale,* by the minuet in the overture to Handel's *Berenice,* and by much eighteenth-century opera.

The third type, the ornamental (corresponding to the "picturesque" in painting), was recognisable by its playful melodic intricacy, its rhythmic perversity, eccentric and difficult harmony, and wild, unexpected modulations. Composers of ornamental music aimed to surprise and delight their audiences, producing music with an immediate impact but no lasting qualities.

The three styles were as basically at variance with each other as, in literature, a chapter of Isiah, a sonnet and an enigma; or, in Grecian architecture, the Doric, Ionic and Corinthian orders.

Nevertheless, Crotch would never have denied that combinations of two or even all three of the categories could frequently be found. Thus, a union of the sublime and the beautiful resulted in "one of the higher walks of our art," typified by much church music, and by madrigals in sixteenth-century style; the alliance of the ornamental style with one of the others "corrects the languor of beauty and the horror of sublimity" and "renders their impression less forcible".

Crotch admitted that individual assessments of composers' music might vary from person to person, but offered his own views on the relative merits of a few of the major figures—views which were founded on a wide knowledge of the repertoire, as is shown by his three volumes of *Specimens of Various Styles of Music,* a collection of short extracts from music by composers as diverse as Guido, Josquin, Tye, Peri, Scarlatti, Handel, J. S. Bach, Clementi, Haydn, Mozart and many others. Complete with commentary on each example, the three volumes show, if nothing else, that the author was a scholar who could claim to be familiar with vast quantities of music both "ancient" (that is, pre-1700) and modern, secular, sacred and in the folksong traditions of various countries; this at a time when very few musicians had much idea of historical perspective or were interested in any but the music of the present moment.

Crotch's views on the earliest experiments in *organum* are, perhaps understandably, scathing: "the barbarous combinations [intervals of 4ths and 5ths] used before the time of Guido do not deserve the name [of harmony]". Josquin, almost five hundred years later, suffers almost as badly: "with whatever veneration we may regard that great luminary of the fifteenth century, and father of harmony, Josquin de Prez, yet, on trying his music, we must own that its merit is rather comparative than positive; his splendour having been greatly eclipsed by the bright constellations of musical excellence which arose in the sixteenth century."

In Dr Crotch's opinion, madrigals and motets of the late seventeenth-century combined sublimity with beauty, but with the cantata came the ornamental style, with vocal melodies "more appropriate to love ditties". On the other hand, the first concertos "contain so much sublimity and beauty, with the ornamental style kept in such due subordination, that we cannot but rank them among the finest works of the art".

For Purcell, Crotch had nothing but praise. His music "has the unfortunate property of making all other music (excepting pure old church music and Bach's organ fugues) appear common and insipid". Crotch set his seal of approval on "the most extra-ordinary genius that this nation ever produced" by asserting that his music was not only sublime but beautiful and ornamental as well, though the latter styles were "not too predominant".

Crotch was introduced late to the music of J. S. Bach. An entry in his *Memoirs,* dated December 1804, admits: "At this time I had not learnt to appreciate Sebn. Bach", and he wrote to Samuel Wesley in 1808, asking for Bach's dates, which the great Bach-enthusiast Wesley could only answer by referring to Karl Friedrich Horn, with whom he was preparing a translation of Forkel's *Über J. S. Bachs Leben, Kunst and Kunstwerke.* Crotch did, however, know the "forty-eight", and he included one of the fugues in the third volume of *Specimens;* probably these were the fugues to which he was referring in an article of 1800, when he claimed: "The only improvement which church music seems to have received in the eighteenth century, was from the organ and other fugues of Handel, which surpass in the subjects themselves, as well as in the manner of treating them, those of Sebastian Bach, Froberger, and every other fuguist".

By the time Crotch came to publish his *Substance of several courses of lectures* in 1831, he had come to know most of Bach's keyboard music, though it is uncertain whether he was acquainted with the major choral works even at this stage. In any case, he felt that he knew enough of Bach's musical output to be able to call him "the Michael Angelo of our art, as Handel was our Raffaelle"; Handel was able to master "every style" of composition, thus making him "the greatest of all musical composers", while for sublimity, Bach was unrivalled.

In referring to contemporary music, Crotch tended to class composers in seemingly haphazard groups of two or three. He mentioned the "frequently magnificent but seldom sublime" choruses of Haydn, Mozart and Beethoven, pointing out, in passing, that the music of these three composers was superior "in originality, genius and science" to that of Pleyel and Kozeluck— a fair comment, shared by all but Crotch's most short-sighted contemporaries. However, the opera overtures of Beethoven, Cherubini and Weber (none of whom is represented by a composition in the *Specimens*) were classed together as "extremely fine and deserving of study", though at another point, it was the overtures of Beethoven, Cherubini and Mozart which were said to demonstrate "the improvement of instrumental full music".

Crotch considered Mozart "the greatest of all modern composers" after hearing his *Requiem,* but he acknowledged the novelty and "gaiety of style" of Haydn's symphonies, which made Haydn "the greatest of all instrumental composers", and noted Beethoven's "original and masterly, frequently sublime" piano music—sublime, though, only "when it does not abound with difficulties of execution". Although Beethoven's symphonies were honoured with the title "wonderful productions", Crotch then implied a contradiction by complaining: "That he, Beethoven, has ever disregarded the rules of composition is to be regretted, and there does not seem to have been the least good obtained by it in any one instance."

Thus Crotch confronted his students with the proposition that in modern music "the instrumental style is greatly advanced, or perhaps arrived at perfection", and that the ornamental style had been cultivated to new heights, all at the expense of the sublime. With the neglect of music's "higher walks", the art was on the decline, and the way to re-introduce the pure sublime into modern music was to study "the mysteries of canon, fugue and imitation", and then imitate the sixteenth-century sacred style in original compositions (a method of teaching which has survived into the late twentieth-century in many universities and music colleges. Crotch recommended the student to model his music on "no one after Greene [1695-1755] or Boyce [1710-1779] ".

He further warned that the student might be disappointed on his first hearing of sublime music, but that he must remember that sublimity "does not strike and surprise, dazzle and amuse, soothe and delight", as does the ornamental. Instead it "elevates and expands the mind". He quoted Sir Joshua Reynolds in his advice to the aspiring composer: "the public requires every thing to be human; and the true artist ought properly to make every thing divine"; and added: "Every period of ten years has some forms or turns of melody peculiar to itself; and which, generally, grow out of fashion before it expires. A composer, who thinks to have his works descend to posterity, must take care to avoid them".

Crotch's theories, though at first sight providing a reasonable basis for musical assessment and criticism, suffered from being too rigid and dogmatic. In the same way that, in the eighteenth century, the tiered social hierarchy was accepted as the natural order, so it seemed logical to Crotch that musical judgement should be based on a similarly compartmentalised structure. Following from such treatment, superlatives (x was the greatest composer; y was the best opera composer), applied to questions which, to twentieth-century minds, can only be judged subjectively, rob many of his arguments of force. Moreover, shortsighted judgements, particularly concerning some aspects of the contemporary musical scene, are now shown in their true light.

On the credit side, Crotch brought his pupils into contact with a wide variety of music, and his scholarship became the basis for much musicological work in the future. As a composer he seems not entirely to have followed through his own theories. Indeed his major works are far from reactionary.

CHAPTER SEVEN

London

D R AND Mrs Crotch now had a young family. Their son,
William Robert, having survived attacks of cowpox and
mumps, caused considerable excitement in 1803 when he was just
four, by playing part of *God save great George our King* on the
harpsichord. However he progressed in a more conventional manner
than had his father, entering Winchester School when he was
thirteen and later becoming ordained.

Of his four sisters, Isabella Martha was the eldest, born in 1800,
while Charlotte Jane (six years Isabella's junior) only survived a
fortnight. Later still, in 1810, twins Jane Catherine and Sarah
Charlotte were born.

During the first five years of the new century, Crotch continued
to direct the Oxford Music Room orchestra, to organise weekly
concerts at St John's College, and to perform in a variety of
benefit concerts for fellow musicians. He carried on giving music
lessons to the local nobility, riding up to twenty miles to give a
lesson, and he took part in weekly private concerts at the home of
Sir Digby Mackworth, where Crotch would sing tenor and play
either the viola or Sir Digby's small chamber organ. A typical
evening's programme was performed on 23rd May, 1804:

Ode to Fancy	William Crotch
Acis and Galatea	Handel
Concerto for organ	
(soloist: Miss Mackworth)	William Crotch
Gloria Patri	
(from *Utrecht Jubilate*)	Handel

Then came supper, followed by the singing of madrigals and glees.
The performers on this occasion were: *Violin I:* Maschall; *Violin II:*
Lloyd; *Viola:* Crotch; *'cello:* Annesley; *Flute I:* Jackson; *Flute II:*
Sir Digby Mackworth; *Organ:* Miss Mackworth; *Sopranos:*
Mesdames Crotch and Ponson; *Alto:* Miller; *Tenor:* Crotch; *Bass:*
Carasmajor.

Oil painting of William Crotch at the age of ten by Sir William Beechey the property
of Royal Academy of Music.   *Piano Publicity Association*

(iii) Engraving entitled "Master Crotch, The Musical

(ii) Crotch aged three from an engraving by James Fittler.

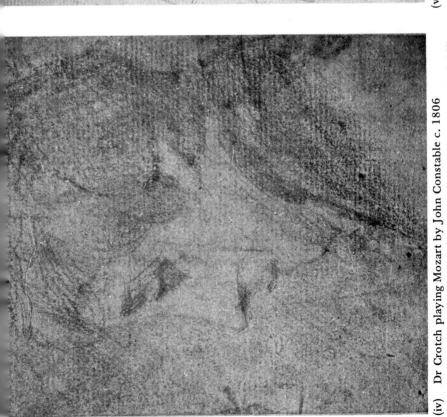

(iv) Dr Crotch playing Mozart by John Constable c. 1806
Norfolk Record Office

(v) Crotch playing the violin by William Delamotte.
Norfolk Record Office

(vii) Crotch self portrait of 1833 in pencil and watercolour.

(vi) William Crotch. A self portrait of 1801 in pencil

(ix) An engraving of 1822 of Dr Crotch by W. T. Fry. *Norfolk Record Office.*

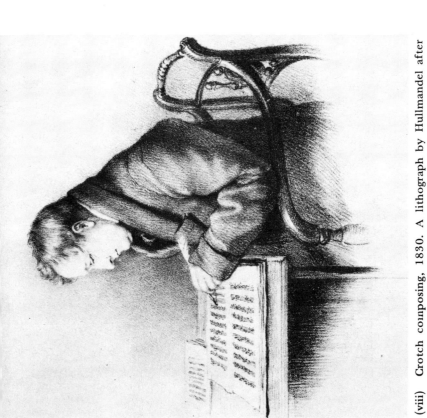

(viii) Crotch composing, 1830. A lithograph by Hullmandel after Mary Anne Pears. *Norfolk Museums Service.*

(xi) Portrait of Crotch's son, W. R. Crotch, as a baby by Gilchrist.
Dr Crotch added the background. *Norfolk Record Office.*

(x) Engraving of Crotch when he had 'flu pub-

Camden Town.
Nov. 25. 1808.

Dear Sir

I hope that I shall always
feel ready to render any Service to the
Cause of real good Musick, & of all those
who are zealous to promote it, among whom
it is known, & acknowledged that you
are eminently conspicuous. In answer to
your Questions concerning the Date of Seb.
Bach's Birth & Decease I cannot at this
Moment give you correctly the Year of either
but it will perhaps be satisfactory News to
inform you that Mr Horn sen.r (the quondam
Instructor of the royal Family) & myself
are preparing for the Press the whole Life
of Sebastian together with an accurate
List of all his Works which much resemble
Handel's for their Multitude & which
(not much to the Honour of England) have
been as yet totally unknown here, even by
their Titles. — This Life was written in
German by Forkel, & has been translated
by Mr Stephenson of Queen Square, a
great Enthusiast in the Cause, & a most
excellent Judge of Musick. — If you however
have any immediate Occasion to be informed
of the exact Dates in Question, I will apply
to Mr Horn, who upon referring to the
Life will be able instantly to satisfy you
concerning them.

First page of Wesley's letter replying to Crotch's query about Bach.
Norfolk Record Office

(xiii) Picture, in pencil and grey wash by Crotch, of the house in Norwich in which
        was born. It was pulled down in 1824.   *Norfolk Museums Servi*

(xiv)   The front parlour, Bedford Place, Kensington by Crotch in 1824.
                                                          Courtauld Institute of A

Despite all these activities, Crotch still had time to keep in touch with old friends such as Charles Hague, who had in 1799 succeeded Randall as Professor of Music in Cambridge. That year also saw Crotch spending much time with Isaac Pring, organist of New College, Oxford, who, though two years his junior, was dying of consumption.

Crotch himself enjoyed, during these years, some of the best health of his life, complaining only of occasional pains in his legs, and toothache, which he used to cure himself by applying nitre (potassium nitrate). On the other hand, he only just avoided a nasty accident on one occasion, when he saw a group of boys twitching hairs out of a horse's tail. Crotch stopped them, but as he walked away, looking back to make sure they had not returned to their former game, he failed to notice an open cellar in his path. He was saved only by the presence of mind of a passer-by (later a friend, Thomas Newbery), who grabbed him and propelled him away from the hole.

More serious was a fall from a short ladder at the Oxford theatre, where Crotch was directing the orchestra. As a result he suffered for a while from pain in what he described as the pit of his stomach.

By 1805, Crotch was appearing more and more frequently in London, visiting friends, playing in concerts, and accompanying services; on at least one occasion, 14th May, he accompanied the service at St Paul's Cathedral, playing for the canticles (Gibbons in F) and Blow's anthem *Bow thine ear*.

The same month he took the solo part in his first organ concerto in a benefit concert for James Bartleman, the bass, whom Crotch had first met at the age of ten; Bartleman had then been fifteen, "his hair about his shoulders", and the leading treble soloist in the Westminster Abbey Choir. Later, Crotch was to write important bass solo parts in his music, designed for Bartleman's flexible and apparently very beautiful voice. In fact, two items which were later included in the oratorio *Palestine* (the bass recitative, *Is this thy place* and the air, *Ye guardian saints*) were first sung by Bartleman in 1804, eight years before the complete work was heard.

That same year, 1804, Crotch and his wife were invited to the Marquis of Buckingham's at Stowe, for three nights of festivities, which included fireworks, parties and a concert. Crotch played his newly-composed *Prelude and Air* on the pianoforte, the Prince Regent seated beside him.

Another cause of Crotch's ever more frequent journeys away from Oxford was his demand as a lecturer on music. In 1804 he was asked to deliver a series of lectures at the Royal Institution in Albemarle Street; in March 1808 he gave six lectures at a Mrs Pope's in Bloomsbury Square, and beginning in April of that year, two series of twelve lectures took place at the Lower Rooms, Hanover Square. For these, he had a class of about two dozen, and amongst them Lady Dartmouth and her daughters, and the violinist Salomon. Samuel Wesley came along to hear what he had to say about J. S. Bach, and was reportedly satisfied.

These lectures were similar to the Oxford ones, though they included new material on such subjects as the theory of sound (acoustics and the mean-tone scale).

In 1801, the growing Crotch family had moved into a house in Holywell, but in January 1805, Crotch decided that his future lay more in the metropolis than in Oxford. He therefore resigned all his Oxford posts except the Professorship, and prepared to leave.

He arranged a farewell benefit music meeting (a series of concerts) in June, which included performances of Handel's *Messiah,* Crotch's own third organ concerto, and his arrangement for voices and orchestra of the *Old Hundredth* hymn-tune.

The actual move to London took place during December, so that the family was settled into lodgings at 43, Great Portland Street in time for Christmas.

Apart from his lectures, Crotch quickly built up a new private teaching practice, raising his fee in 1807 from 10/6d. a quarter to 15/- (for "professors"—his term for professional musicians) or a guinea (for amateurs).

On his annual visit to Cambridge to see his mother in the summer of 1807, Crotch performed a considerable feat. Playing the organ at Charles Hague's music meeting for performances of both *Judas Maccabæus* and *The Creation,* it was discovered that the organ was below orchestral pitch. He therefore transposed the whole of both works up a semitone at sight.

The year 1808 saw two removals. In June the Crotch family moved round the corner, from Great Portland Street into number two Duchess Street; but a greater upheaval took place in Norwich, where William's father sold the old family home, in which both of them had been born, and went to live in St Clement's Church Yard. The house in Green's Lane was pulled down a few years later.

Crotch visited Oxford every summer, to take part in concerts and formal functions which required the presence of the Professor. During the 1810 visit he played an organ concerto at the second concert of a four-day music meeting, while both his glee *Mona on Snowdon calls* and the bass aria *Ye guardian saints* were performed at the third.

Family life must have taken much of Crotch's time, with the birth of twin daughters, the addition to the household of a dog called Gioco, whom Crotch considered both faithful and sensible, and his wife's nervous fever which, in 1809, caused all her hair to drop out, seemingly as a result of shock at the death of a close relative. From this time until her death, she complained of almost-constant "face-ache".

CHAPTER EIGHT

Palestine

THE Doctor's many commitments left him little time for composition. Nevertheless, the work for which he is best remembered, the oratorio *Palestine,* was completed in 1812 and first performed at the Hanover Square Rooms on 21st April. The overflowing audience was so enthusiastic that the work was repeated on 26th May, and parties came from both Oxford and Cambridge to hear it.

It was heard again on 5th April the following year, and full performances took place at an Oxford music meeting in 1820 (Bartleman died on the way home after singing the bass solo part written for him), at the Hanover Square Rooms in 1827 and 1828, in Worcester (1827 and 1833), and in Oxford (1827), Hereford (1840) and Hull (1840); and on 5th March 1823, when it was given at the Theatre Royal, Drury Lane, with Sir George Smart conducting, it received such acclaim that it was repeated on the 12th, and then again on the 21st. Selections from the work were heard in concerts for many years, and certain numbers entered the cathedral repertory as anthems, where they still retain their place.

By the standards of the early nineteenth-century, this was popularity indeed; Handel's choral works were still performed (mainly at music festivals and at the oratorio concerts which replaced secular opera in the Covent Garden Opera House on two nights a week during Lent), but even these were rarely heard in full. A writer in *Quarterly Musical Magazine and Review* (in 1818), deploring the public's lack of interest in full-scale oratorios, said that these works "are voted dull and heavy, and selections have almost entirely superseded them, while to the eye and ear of musical erudition they can never fail to exhibit the strongest concentration of the powers of genius and learning". Thus it was that the few English oratorios which had appeared since Samuel Arnold's *Prodigal Son* (1773) and James Hook's *The Ascension* (1776)—works by such composers as King, Perry, Russell and Cudmore—were received without enthusiasm and tended to be quickly forgotten. All the more surprising, then, that *Palestine* was given such a warm welcome.

After all, Crotch, in modelling *Palestine* according to the old rules, was not aiming for popularity in a London entirely subservient to continental trends in musical taste. He held up the *sublime* in music as his constant goal, and it was because he wished to demonstrate his disapproval of current *ornamental* music that he chose to use the form of composition which had housed the supremely sublime masterpieces of Handel.

Crotch carefully selected his libretto from a poem by Reginald Heber (later Bishop of Calcutta and author of the words to the hymns *Holy, holy, holy* and *From Greenland's icy mountains*), after he had heard it in 1803, the year it won the Oxford medal for English poetical composition. It has no cohesive "plot" but is a disquisition on the history of Palestine, from the reigns of David and Solomon to the coming of Christ.

There are some superbly dramatic lines, but it is nevertheless easy to sympathise with the newspaper critic Anthony Hicks, who wrote of the poem's "dreary couplets, periphrases and hackneyed epithets"; the tone of much of the language can be appreciated if one quotes the first eight lines of the bass air (number 20):

> "For thee his ivory load Behemoth bore,
> And far Sofala teem'd with golden ore;
> Thine all the arts that wait on wealth's increase,
> Or bask and wanton in the beam of peace.
>
> When Tiber slept beneath the cypress gloom,
> And silence held the lonely woods of Rome;
> Or ere to Greece the builder's skill was known,
> Or the light chisel brush'd the Parian stone;"

But however indigestible the words may seem today, they provided the composer with the inspiration for a masterly piece of music.

The oratorio is divided into two roughly equal sections lasting a total of more than two-and-a-half hours, which, with the addition of an interval, brings the performing time to three hours. The scoring is for four-part chorus and semi-chorus, three soloists (soprano or treble, tenor and bass) and a large orchestra of strings, flute, oboes, bassoons, horns, two trumpets, three trombones, timpani, solo clarinet (which would originally have been played by the leader of the orchestra), harp and continuo (the keyboard part of which might have been taken by either piano or organ, though the latter is more effective).

Bearing in mind Handel's considerable influence on Crotch, particularly through the enthusiasm of his teachers—Professor Randall at Cambridge, Professor Hayes at Oxford—it would be reasonable to expect *Palestine* to be, if not a blind imitation of the German composer's musical style, at least a logical development from it. Indeed, Crotch's intense admiration for Handel had been expressed in 1809, the fiftieth anniversary of the latter's death, when he gave an organ recital of his own arrangements for keyboard of Handel's music in the Hanover Square Rooms.

But despite Crotch's championing of Handel, the oratorio *Palestine* defies arbitrary stylistic categorisation. To comprehend its significance, one must analyse aspects of the form and style of the music, beginning with a table outlining the work's basic structure:

Number (Novello octavo ed., not ms. numbering)	Title	Category	Key(s)
PART ONE			
1	Overture		C,c,C
2	"Reft of thy sons"	Air and Chorus	c
3	"Is this thy place"	Bass recit.	f-e
4	"Ye guardian saints"	Bass air	C
5	"O happy once"	Chorus	F
6	"But now thy sons"	Tenor air and chorus	d
7	"O thou, their guide"	Treble air	D
8	"Oh, feeble boast"	Chorus	D
9	"Let Sinai tell"	Chorus	d
10	"But who shall dare"	Bass recit.	d-Bb
11	"Awe-struck I cease"	Bass air	F
12	"Such were the cares"	Treble recit.	Bb-Eb
13	"Triumphant race"	Treble air	Eb
14	"And he, the kingly sage"	Tenor recit.	Ab-D
15	"To him were known"	Tenor air	D
16	"Hence all his might"	Chorus	G
17	"Yet e'en the works"	Treble recit.	E
18	"In frantic converse"	Treble air and semi-chorus	E
19	"Such, the faint echo"	Treble/tenor duet	A
20	"For thee his iv'ry load"	Bass air	F
21	"No workman steel"	Bass recit. (acc.)	C
22	"Then the harp awoke"	Bass air and chorus	C

23	"Did Israel shrink"	Tenor air	G
24	"E'en they who dragg'd"	Treble air	b
25	"Nor vain their hope"	Chorus	D
26	"Lo! star-led chiefs"	Quartet	G
27	"Daughter of Sion"	Chorus	A
28	"He comes"	Chorus	D
29	"Be peace on earth"	Quartet and chorus	D
30	"Thou palsied earth"	Bass recit. (acc.)	d-f
31	"Are those his limbs"	Bass air and chorus	f-F
32	"Ye faithful few"	Treble air	d
33	"Vengeance! thy fiery wing"	Tenor air	Bb
34	"But heavier far"	Bass recit. (acc.)	c
35	"Ah, fruitful now no more"	Bass air	Eb
36	"Then on your tops"	Quartet and chorus	F
37	"No more your thirsty rocks"	Treble air	C
38	"And who is he?/ To highest heaven"	Bass air	G
39	"Lo! cherub bands"	'Sestett'	E
40	"And shall not Israel's sons"	Treble recit. (acc.)	D
41	"Hosanna!"	Chorus	D
42	"Worthy the lamb"	Chorus	D
43	"Hallelujah! Amen"	Chorus	D

To oversimplify the work's plan, it is true to say that in many cases a loud, fast chorus will be followed by a quiet, flowing air (a word used by the composer in preference to the Italian "aria"), and this will, in turn, lead to a modulatory recitative and another air (this time loud). The basic key-scheme shows predominantly conservative tonal progressions and relationships between numbers (major to relative minor; tonic to dominant; and tonic to subdominant, for example).

The exceptions are therefore all the more unexpected and striking, and particularly the mediant relationships which introduce a Romantic approach unexpected in an English composer as early as 1812. There are in fact four occasions on which a number begins in the mediant of the key in which the previous number ended, and six instances of a new number beginning either a tone above or a tone below its predecessor. In only three cases does a recitative cushion the effect of the change.

The reason for such procedures seems, in every case, to be closely concerned with the argument of the text, with a relaxation or a tightening of the tension. Thus in *Ye faithful few* (no. 32), the nostalgic "weep for your country, weep for your children" is suddenly plunged, by means of a leap from D minor to B flat major, into a determined cry for "Vengeance!" (no. 33). Not only is the tonality wrenched from its foundations; the pulse alters from a 3/2 largo movement to a 4/4 presto, and the treble soloist hands over to the more powerful tenor.

Similar reflection of the text can be discerned in varied orchestral textures. The rushing string semiquavers of *Did Israel Shrink* (no. 23), which aptly portray "the raging deep" and "billows of the proud", are replaced in the following number, the quiet, sad treble air, *E'en they who dragg'd,* by a delicate accompaniment which uses solo oboe, harp, horns and strings.

Fascinating also is the use made of the two clarinets, which were still not accepted, at this time, as legitimate members of an orchestra. In *Palestine* they are used very sparingly; to provide additional dark colour to the words "Are those his limbs, with ruthless scourges torn" (no. 31); in *Vengeance!* (no. 32), where a 'rasping' early-clarinet sound played as a solo above the strings adds 'bite' to the texture; and in both the overture and the chorus *Then the harp awoke,* in which the clarinets are distributed in much the same manner as the oboes.

It is evident that, despite its deficiencies, the poem provided Crotch with the catalyst which set in motion his creativity. Even the words "Then on your tops" are set to a triplet figure which evokes a sense of 'joie de vivre' appropriate to the text, while there are a number of occasions when mere word-painting and scene-setting reach heights of understanding which could only result from the composer's thorough sympathy with the words.

Perhaps the most arresting example of this is the chorus *Let Sinai Tell,* whose portrayal of "the red mountain like a furnace" and the "whirlwind" and "darkness", makes use of full orchestra (including trombones, timpani and organ) in two extended arches, whose dynamics and tessitura shift dramatically alongside one another, using suspensions and modulations which show Crotch in a very different light from the reactionary theorist who only looked to the past for musical greatness. The long trills of the opening bars set the mood of the whole chorus with an intangible feeling of restlessness:

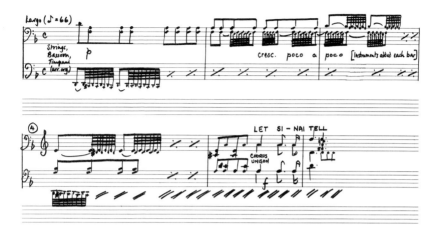

It is sobering to read, in an article on "English Ecclesiastical Composers of the Present Age" by H. J. Gauntlett (*The Musical World,* ii, 21; 5.8.1836), the author's scathing criticism of this chorus. He refers to essential harmonies treated as mere passing notes, leaving the chord imperfect: "To our ears the position, as it stands in the vocal score copy with the arranged accompaniment by the composer, is perfectly intolerable". However, the writer in *Quarterly Musical Magazine and Review* (i, 488; 1818) wrote that this number carried "the sublime in music to its acme".

Crotch used chromatic movement elsewhere, for depicting "grief", "shame" and "sorrow", and for pictorial effects such as the colouring of "the mournful wind" (no. 18):

The chromatic passing notes in the inner parts of the accompaniment in the tenor air *But now thy sons* (no. 6), beneath the words "remorse and shame", are almost anticipations of passages of Elgar:

The quartet *Lo! star-led chiefs* (no. 26), which still makes frequent appearances in cathedral service lists (usually sung by full choir with organ accompaniment) gains considerably by being performed as originally intended. The contrasts between strings and wind (with the horns reaching their top notes) are most effective, and the passing-notes which give the piece much of its character are heard more distinctly in the orchestra than on an organ.

Perhaps one of the least subtle, though by no means inappropriate pieces of musical imagery comes in the air *Then the harp awoke* (no. 22), in which the harp literally plays interludes on its own; and incidentally, a cynic might be tempted to see here the influence of a very similar idea in Haydn's *The Creation:*

—and in Handel's *Judas Maccabæus,* a comparable passage is set for chorus to the words "Tune your harps".

A similar piece of imagery explains the two strokes of the timpani at "the cymbal clang'd" (presumably Crotch would have used a cymbal, had one been available); and a different form of word-painting appears in the chorus *Worthy the lamb,* in which the words "who died" (sung *piano*) are followed on each appearance by "who lived" (sung *forte*).

This chorus (no. 42) is undoubtedly indebted to Handel's *Messiah* for its opening phrase:

though this is where the similarity ends. The crotchets:

provide a useful countersubject which is used at various points by each of the voices and by the orchestra in the overall contrapuntal texture. The final *Hallelujah* chorus which follows, also contrapuntally conceived, is a grand affair, very much in the Handelian tradition.

One can play a diverting little game with *Palestine,* tracing its multiplicity of styles to their roots in other composers' music. Thus one can see a parallel between the fiery tenor air *But now thy sons* (no. 6) and the *allegro moderato* section of *Now vanish before the holy beams* (Haydn's *The Creation*):

The loud unison opening of the duet *Such, the faint echo* (no. 19) is reminiscent of a favourite procedure of Haydn:

—though the graceful elegance of the rest of this duet seems to recall J. C. Bach and the Pleasure Gardens composers.

However, the "bogus" cadence leading from the accompanied recitative *But heavier far* (no. 34) into the air *Ah! Fruitful now no more* strikes one almost as a gesture of defiance against the established conventions:

Violino Secondo part for the bass air *Ye Guardian Saints*, from *Palestine*, in Crotch's hand. *Norfolk Record Office.*

The opening bars of *Lo! star-led chiefs* from *Palestine*, in its original orchestral version. A copy in Crotch's hand. *Royal Academy of Music.*

Palestine opens with a French Overture, and proceeds to show influences from a wide variety of sources (and they certainly are influences and not plagiarisms). It would of course be unrealistic to ignore this stylistic reliance on others. On the other hand, it would be equally short-sighted to overlook those sparks of originality which transform so many numbers into very personal modes of expression.

Nor must one ever be allowed to forget the sound craftsmanship of Crotch's orchestral scoring; a point often forgotten by critics who have not heard the music and who judge the work from the vocal score arrangement. Similarly the treatment of both chorus and solo writing proves the composer's practical understanding of the human voice.

One of the oratorio's major drawbacks is its excessive length; another is its apparent lack of cohesion. The absence of tautness in the poem, itself the main cause of the length problem, must also be blamed for the inclusion of some musical items of doubtful value, which could well be omitted from modern revivals.

Shortened versions of *Palestine* are in fact entirely palatable to a modern audience, and they prove that English music of the early nineteenth-century, though rightly considered a desert, did boast at least one oasis. And indeed, a fairly summary look at the rest of Crotch's musical output makes it absolutely clear that the arid wastes were not actually as barren as some musical historians would have us believe.

CHAPTER NINE

Royal Academy of Music

IN LONDON, teaching took more and more of Crotch's time. From 1812 till 1823 he gave annual courses of lectures at the Surrey Institution, and his private teaching practice became his main source of income.

He continued to visit both Oxford and Cambridge every year, and to take part in concerts in London and elsewhere. Thus in August 1813, he played the organ at the opening of the Military College at Sandhurst before a company which included the Queen, the Prince Regent, and the Dukes of York, Clarence, Cambridge, Norfolk and Brunswick, Crotch was particularly proud of his position at the console in the centre of one gallery, directly opposite the Queen who sat in the centre of the other.

In a concert in London, Samuel Wesley and Crotch played a duet which Wesley had written, but it would be difficult to prove either that this was the famous *Duett for the Organ* (of 1812) or that this performance pre-dated that in which Wesley was partnered by Vincent Novello in the Hanover Square Rooms.

On his Oxford visit in 1812, Crotch saw the now-dying Malchair for the last time, and the following year two more deaths occurred—those of Crotch's own father in Norwich, and of Dr Jowett (of Trinity Hall, Cambridge).

Not all was serious in Crotch's life at this time, however, and it is a relief to discover that in 1812 he put on a performance with puppets of *Henry V* together with John Constable (whom he had met in 1806), who painted one of the scenes. Then, when the Thames froze over during the severe winter of 1813-1814, he attended the fair held on it, and crossed over the Serpentine, while his wife walked over the ice above Putney Bridge. He was also to be seen at the regular fireworks displays at Parson's Green and in Hyde Park.

In Oxford in 1814, his Professorial duties were brought into question when he organised a small orchestra to play in the theatre at a performance attended by the Prince Regent, the Emperor of Russia, the King of Prussia, the Chancellor of the University, the Duchess of Oldenburgh, and the Mayor and Bailiff of Oxford. The players struck up but were hushed into silence. "Dr Crotch", cried a voice. "Sir!" he replied. "There must be no music as long as the Duchess of Oldenburgh is in the theatre as she cannot bear it". "Very well, sir", agreed the Professor, who had no choice but to watch the musicless performance together with his redundant orchestra.

The Crotch family twice moved house during this period, first to a cottage in Bishop's Grove, Fulham, in 1813 (though for a while Crotch continued to teach at Duchess Street), and in 1815, to North End, Fulham, to a house with an 83-feet Lombardy poplar in the garden for which Crotch had great affection. One of Crotch's interests was church architecture, and it is thus not surprising that he made a point of visiting many of the churches in the vicinity of their new homes. One which particularly impressed him was the Park Chapel, originally built in 1718, but when Crotch visited it, just rebuilt (it was pulled down and replaced in 1910 by St Andrew's, Park Walk, S.W.10).

Another chapel which figured importantly in Crotch's life from about 1812 onwards was the Surrey Chapel (whose minister, the Rev. Rowland Hill, though Evangelistic, nevertheless encouraged good music). Benjamin Jacob, the organist there, with the help of both Wesley and Crotch, gave a series of organ recitals mainly of excerpts from oratorios (airs, choruses and fugues). Handel's works naturally featured prominently, but excerpts from *Palestine* regularly appeared.

For two years (1815 and 1816), Crotch conducted the annual concert in St Paul's Cathedral "for the sons of the clergy", but he resigned the position because of the intolerable system of orchestral deputising, which resulted in the appearance of one orchestra for the rehearsal and another for the performance. He was succeeded by Thomas Greatorex, who was to become Organist of Westminster Abbey in 1819.

Each year, Mrs Crotch and the children went away on holiday for up to two months, and it was on their visit to Chichester in 1818 that she broke her arm running down the Bishop's garden. But it was not serious, and in August her husband was able to leave her to visit Cambridge, where Charles Hague showed him the

Fitzwilliam Collection of musical manuscripts, and the two Professors spent much of their time together playing bowls.

The early 1820's was a period always remembered by Crotch as a time of family mourning. First, in August 1820, little Gioco died at the age of fourteen; then in January 1821, the Crotches' eldest daughter Isabella died. Her father's obituary shows with what sorrow he accepted this blow: "Our dear daughter Isabella died in the faith, at ye age of 20; her whole life was a blessing to us, as we doubt not her death has been to herself".

A lasting memorial to her took the form of the house at Kensington Gravel Pits (now part of the Bayswater Road), which Isabella had chosen just before her death, and which became the Crotch family's new home in May 1821.

* *

In 1822, Lord Burghersh (later Lord Westmorland), an amateur composer of seven full-scale Italian operas and a good deal of Anglican church music, asked Crotch to be the first Principal of his new Royal Academy of Music, and Crotch agreed.

The Academy started life at number four, Tenterden Street, Hanover Square, as a boarding school for not more than forty girls and forty boys, who were admitted between the ages of ten and fifteen, and were to be trained to become professional musicians. The constitution at the foundation required that the Principal should be "a person of character and repute....to whom shall be entrusted the general direction of the musical education of the students", and he had to help him a staff of distinguished musicians, including (on the Board of Professors) the organists of St Paul's and Westminster Abbey (Thomas Attwood and Thomas Greatorex), William Shield (the composer and violinist) and Sir George Smart (conductor, composer and an organist of the Chapel Royal). In addition, twenty-nine other professors included Sir Henry Bishop (opera-conductor and composer), Muzio Clementi (virtuoso pianist and composer), Dragonetti (the double-bass player), Robert Lindley (the 'cellist) and Cipriani Potter (Crotch's former pupil and eventual successor). Crotch, apart from directing overall policy and dealing with much of the administration of the new institution, also taught harmony and counterpoint.

Sir William Sterndale Bennett entered the Academy in 1826, just before his tenth birthday, and studied composition with

Crotch. He remembered: "An active man, he used to walk from his house in the neighbourhood of Campden Hill to Tenterden Street, entering his classroom with his pockets distended by paint-boxes and sketch-books, and allowing his pupils, to their great delight, to examine any additions he had made on his walk through Kensington Gardens. A musical treat, often enjoyed by his class, was his playing from memory a series of the Choruses of Handel, which he could select with endless variety."

Crotch believed strongly that his pupils should master the elements of composition before progressing onto new ground. Thus Bennett was made to write double chants while privately, and without his teacher's knowledge, he was experimenting with a string quartet modelled on those of Mozart. Though firm in his beliefs, Crotch was in fact also tolerant of other approaches to teaching by individual professors; indeed, the Academy's constitution laid down that "Each professor, called upon to teach in the academy, shall instruct according to his own system."

Dr Crotch conducted the inaugural concert of the Royal Academy in the Opera House, Covent Garden, on St George's Day, 1823 (the date chosen to honour the institution's patron, King George IV), and the programme included extracts from *Palestine.* The following February Crotch organised a concert in aid of the Academy, which included a performance of his *Ode on the King's Accession,* which he had first conducted in Oxford in 1821.

This time, however, the performers were the Academy's own pupils, and indeed this was their first public appearance. According to contemporary critics, the star performer was Henry Blagrove, the violinist, then aged twelve, who led the orchestra and played a solo. Apart from the *Ode,* there were pieces by Haydn, Marcello, Dussek, Zingarelli, Bochsa, Viotti, Sarti, Hummel, Mayer and Duport, for orchestra and choir, 'cello, oboe and voice, piano duet, and a trio for harp, piano and 'cello. Apparently the standard of performance was high.

As Principal, Crotch was determined that his pupils should hear music at its best, be instructed by the leading musicians of the time, and be encouraged to imitate their examples. So in 1826 there took place a series of six vocal and instrumental concerts by leading performers, the second of which was attended by Weber. In his honour, the programme included his overture to *Beherrscher der Geister* and an Italian song (probably opus 50, the *Misera me* for soprano), and this must have been one of the last occasions on which the composer heard his own music; he died less than two months later.

As an integral part of their training, the students at the Academy were also encouraged to perform their own compositions in special pupils' concerts—an idea of Crotch's which proved most beneficial, and which has been practised at music colleges ever since.

Proof of Crotch's good relationship with his young pupils comes with a round which he composed. Entitled *The Academy Roll Call to Dinner,* and dated 1826, it includes in its text the names (in pun-form) of his pupils, and was doubtless sung by them all.

Crotch later wrote: "I now *reigned* at ye Academy and had as much good music performed as I could—nevertheless mine was a *limited* monarchy". Indeed, the Academy was in severe financial difficulties, and no doubt its Committee of Management was not particularly generous with extra grants for specific projects.

Money was not the only cause of contention. Lord Burghersh irritated Crotch by continually pressing him to mount concerts of Italian opera, including his own; and the President and his Principal disagreed over the question of female pupils being allowed to appear on the stage. A letter from Dr Crotch, dated 11th October 1830, summarises the situation, and points to Crotch's happier relations with his pupils than with his employers:

"My Lord,

      I have received through the Revd. Mr Hamilton your Lord-ship's message complaining of my having endeavoured to persuade the female students of the Royal Academy to refuse compliance with the requirements of the Committee who had fully discussed the subject of their appearing as chorus singers on the stage, and determined that there was no impropriety in their doing so. That if masters were to act thus it would be impossible for the committee to carry its plans into effect for the improvement of the Academy. And that instead of addressing the pupils I should have made my complaint to the Committee.

      My only reason for not doing so, my Lord, was that I felt conscious that I had never concealed my sentiments on the subject from the committee.

Not long after the opening of the Academy, when the Count St Antonio, who was then the only member of the Committee in town, made the first proposal of the kind, I felt it my duty, as Principal, to state to him in a letter my individual opinion, an opinion in which I do not stand alone though I may not have a majority on my side, which was that it would eventually be highly injurious to the Academy and was contrary to the wills of the generality of respectable English Parents. The experiment was given up and not resumed for a considerable time.

But I beg, through your Lordship as Chairman, to assure the Committee that, as a master, I can have no wish to frustrate their plans for the improvement of the Academy; and to state most distinctly that in the present instance the reluctance which the females have shown to going on the stage has not originated in my interference. Two or three of them, indeed, who were already decidedly averse to the proposal have asked my advice confidentially, and that I have, of course given frankly, which in all cases was that the individual should act according to the dictates of her own conscience.

My Lord, I have the honour to remain,
Your Lordship's obliged and obedient Servant,
William Crotch."

Little more than a year later, Dr Crotch was having further difficulties involving the female students. The Academy's minute book records the following entry on 8th December 1831: "The Committee having received a Report of the manner in which the Harmony Lessons in the Female Department were conducted by Dr Crotch, which was extremely unsatisfactory, they resolved that his future attendance on the Female Students should henceforth be dispensed with." The following week, on 15th December, one terse sentence ended Crotch's reign at the Academy: "Read a letter from Dr Crotch stating that it is his Intention to resign his Situation as Principal, and Professor of Harmony, at Midsummer next."

The reason for this hurried departure was apparently that Dr Crotch had indiscreetly rewarded one of the girls for a particularly brilliant harmony exercise, by giving her a kiss. At that very moment, Mrs Iliff, the Academy's governess, had happened to enter the room, and not being accustomed to seeing her girls embraced by their professors, had at once submitted an agitated report to the Committee. This body, entirely misunderstanding her account of the affair, and perhaps looking for an excuse to rid themselves of Crotch, passed that damning resolution which forced him to resign.

CHAPTER TEN

The Decline

DURING his years at the Royal Academy, Crotch had by no means restricted his activities to Tenterden Street.

Between 1820 and 1833, he gave twelve courses of lectures at the Royal Institution, and courses at both the London Institution, Moorfields, and the London Literary and Scientific Institution. He occasionally conducted the Philharmonic concerts in London, in addition to his conducting in Oxford at many of the music meetings. His income was augmented yet further by his almost invariable insistence that at any performance of *Palestine,* he should not only conduct but be paid two hundred guineas for the loan of the unpublished instrumental parts.

The year 1826 saw the death of the Crotches' daughter Sarah Charlotte, despite a visit made with her mother to Richmond to recover in the country air. Within six years, her twin-sister Jane Catharine was also dead. Two other deaths in the immediate family were less unexpected; those of Crotch's elder brother Michael (in 1826), and his mother (in 1830), the latter having survived well into her nineties.

It was during this period of successive bereavements that Crotch's own health began to deteriorate. He put on weight, his old knee-trouble confined him to bed for days at a time, and he began to complain of back-ache. To make matters worse, when he did walk he had a habit of tripping and spraining an already weak ankle.

The man who was forced to leave the Academy in disgrace was middle-aged (fifty-six when he resigned) and ill. Evidently he felt that his life's work was behind him, since one of his first tasks was the sorting-out (and in many cases, the destroying) of piles of papers and letters which had collected over the years. These he used as a basis for his *Memoirs*—a manuscript volume now in Norwich, in which he recorded the version of his life story which he considered most appropriate for public consumption. Most of the facts and dates (though not all) are accurate, but perhaps more interesting are the omissions; there is, for example, no mention of the resignation from the Academy.

The volume relies heavily, for details of its author's early childhood, on the printed accounts by Burney and Daines Barrington, while the section devoted to the later childhood includes long quotations from a manuscript in Crotch's possession, written by Schomberg and entitled *Some Memoirs of the early life of William Crotch.* Crotch's version, however, as he admits, leaves out "repetitions and a few circumstances that I am quite aware he never meant should be seen by any eyes except my own"; and the original version would appear to have been destroyed.

Unfortunately, Crotch's own opinions are rarely to be found in his *Memoirs,* though occasionally one finds an addition made by the author on reading through a page some years after it had been written; thus an entry for January 1812, referring to his son, has a later addition in brackets: "Wm. went to Winchester School. A comet visible (but I do not say in consequence)". A similar entry for October 1816 adds hindsight: "Mrs Lushington's House near Croydon was struck [by lightning]. Ann B. was there, in the very house (and it so altered her constitution as to do her great benefit)".

Once the *Memoirs* had reached the present (1832-3), they became little more than a calendar of visits and astronomical observations, together with annual lists of Crotch's pupils.

Crotch may by this time have been on the decline, but he refused to admit defeat. He moved in October 1832 to lodgings at number ten, Holland Road, Kensington, where he would have long conversations over tea with the landlord, Mr Cox, mainly about painting and religion. On Cox's death in 1835, Crotch was highly complimentary about his Indian ink sketches, his oil landscapes and his original groups of figures: "We endeavoured to adopt each other's styles, but his illness prevented complete success". However, Crotch did not endorse Cox's religious views with such fervour: "His religion was superintended by a New-Jerusalem priest of the Swedenborghian kind. He lent me a book in wch. the persons of ye Holy Trinity exist not altogether but first the Father, secondly the Son and thirdly the Holy Spirit, which I cannot but think *heresy!*"

Similar subjects were discussed every Friday evening, when Crotch and a group of friends (chiefly Smalley, Newbery, Mudie, Drummond and Captain Caldwell) met to talk and make music. Calling themselves "The Club", they began to meet regularly in 1831 (usually at Crotch's house), and they can be seen as an extension of "The Great School", the group of mainly amateur artists of which first Malchair, and then Crotch, had been President.

Sometimes the Club's music-making would be almost entirely instrumental, as on 23rd January 1835, when it included fugues by Crotch, a symphony by Haydn, some Beethoven sonatas and excerpts from the second version of *Captivity of Judah;* or on 23rd March 1835, when they played a duet arrangement of the overture to *Fidelio* (which was encored) and two sonatas by Beethoven "with violin accompaniments", finishing with some of Barnett's songs. At others it would be mainly vocal, as on 15th June 1835, when two Haydn symphonies were followed by anthems by Gibbons, Purcell, Batten, Goldwin, Creighton, Croft and Child (each performed twice) and ending with some new psalm tunes by Crotch.

In later life Crotch became ever more devout, so that when he was well enough, he regularly attended the Bayswater Chapel—as worshipper or occasionally as organist. His son, now headmaster of the grammar school at Taunton, frequently visited London, and would sometimes preach in the chapel.

Crotch also attended Miss Fryer's musical evenings, perhaps once every two or three months, to take part in *ad hoc* performances—rather like some Club evenings, one imagines—of choral works such as *Palestine* and *Captivity of Judah.* A typical rendering would be given by a choir of about twenty voices, accompanied on two pianos, or by one piano and a couple of violins.

Crotch managed to leave London on a number of occasions during 1833 and 1834. He visited friends and relatives in Taunton, Bath, Salisbury, Portsmouth, Sidmouth and Chichester in 1833, and the following June he was in Oxford for the Installation of the Duke of Wellington as Chancellor of the University. For the occasion he had composed an ode, to a libretto by Keble, "When these are days of old", and at the same festival there took place the first performance of the final version of *Captivity of Judah.* At the first full rehearsal, on 7th June in the Music Room, Crotch sprained his ankle yet again, but he was fit enough to conduct both the final rehearsal on the 9th and the performance on 10th June.

Returning to London on 16th June, following three days of concerts, Crotch then prepared for what turned out to be his last important public appearance, at the Handel Festival in Westminster Abbey. There was a rehearsal on 27th, and the following day Crotch directed the concert from the specially-erected organ.

This was the last period in which Crotch enjoyed even reasonably good health. In November 1835 he had a "shaking fit" one night, and blisters swelled up all over his right leg. Sir Benjamin Brodie, a leading surgeon who attended him, "punctured the instep in fifteen places with a thing like a needle", as Crotch put it. To cure the deep imposthume (or abscess) which remained, he was prescribed a lotion of brandy and water, and an intake of food every two hours. It was not till Christmas Day that he sat up for the first time, and it took another fortnight before he was able to dress.

For the whole of 1836 Crotch was wheeled about in a wheelchair, drawn by an old man called Cook. Only in April the following year did he begin to walk again.

In July 1836, Dr and Mrs Crotch moved home again, this time to Camden Villas, Bedford Place, Kensington, and in November there arrived a small pipe-organ which Crotch had ordered from Bishop, the Norwich organ-builder. The next year saw both the addition to this organ of a drum-stop and the arrival of a new pianoforte; and in 1846, a further double-drum was added to the organ. It is now impossible to know whether or not the small organ in the possession of Christ Church Cathedral, Oxford, which is purported to have been built by Crotch, is in fact the instrument built for him by Bishop.

Crotch had great affection for his grandchildren, as was shown when little Edmund died in Taunton of a "bowel attack" just before his third birthday; Crotch described him as "a remarkably sweet child". He must have been a popular grandpa; at any rate, he spent many hours devising games for his grandchildren, and in 1838 he wrote a miniature encyclopaedia for William Duppa, then aged nearly six, entitled: *Hotchpogeology—or a little of the CREAM OF KNOWLEDGE Skimmed off for the breakfast of VERY YOUNG or VERY IGNORANT PERSONS, BY THE VERY WORTHY, THE PRESIDENT OF THE GREAT SCHOOL—1838—KENSINGTON*. The knowledge ranges from astronomy to mechanics, chronology to chemistry, descriptions and drawings of cathedrals to an explanation of gas lights.

It is almost as exhaustive as *The Road to Learning,* a volume bound in green morocco which Crotch began writing in 1795 and was still adding to in 1838. The first eight subjects in the alphabetical index give an idea as to the work's scope: Abridgement of the Bible; Anatomy; Apochrypha; Architecture; Arithmetic; Astronomy; Bellringing; Botany. Other subjects include Electricity, Fencing, Fortifications and Optics, the last being an explanation of a method invented by the author of finding the magnifying power of a telescope.

In his final years Crotch continued to make arrangements of symphonic works for pianoforte solo and piano duet; he published in 1842 his *Rules for Chanting the Psalms;* and in 1838 he composed his anthem for chorus and orchestra *The Lord is King,* which was performed in Exeter Hall on 10th March 1843. He continued to take private pupils, calculating that he had taught almost nine hundred by 1844; and he continued both making astronomical observations and drawing and painting.

But his bad health not only made work difficult; it considerably reduced Crotch's potential income. Thus when Samuel Wesley's daughter wrote in 1838, asking if he would consider subscribing to her father's motet *Confitebor,* he refused, with the comment (written in the third person): "He wishes Miss Wesley better success with the affluent", though he would be willing to have his name mentioned, if that should be of any use.

He also laid down a strange rule during the early 1830's, that he would no longer provide anybody with a testimonial. Thus, although he was a personal friend of the Wesley family, and had given Wesley's daughter various presents over the years (for instance, a copy of his *Elements of Musical Composition,* and a transcription specially intended for her album, together with his "sincerest wishes for success"), he nevertheless refused to write her a testimonial when she requested one.

Since the Academy resignation, Crotch had in fact been constantly on the defensive. And hardly surprisingly, considering some of the criticism he was receiving in the musical press.

In 1832 the Gresham Prize "for the best original composition in sacred vocal music" was inaugurated, the three adjudicators being Crotch, William Horsley (organist and composer of both psalm-tunes and secular glees and songs) and Richard Stevens (organist of the Temple Church and a composer of glees). The prize was established in order that "....ecclesiastical music would resume its influence, and extend its circle of admirers" at a time when most musicians agreed that church music was at a low ebb. Crotch himself had written: "I should indeed rejoice, if all compositions less than a century old were at present excluded from the Church service. Few productions of the present day will ever become fit for divine service at all."

The results of the competition, when they were announced, caused considerable controversy, as can be judged from extracts from an article in *The Musical World* (II, 19, p. 81; II, 20, p. 97) by H. J. Gauntlett; referring to the entrants whose compositions had been judged in the first five places (Charles Hart, Kellow Pye, John Goss, George Elvey and Charles Lucas), Gauntlett comments: "It will be seen, that two of these gentlemen are professors of harmony and composition in the Royal Academy; and with the exception of one, all have more or less experienced the high advantage of studying the creed adopted by the learned professor for the University of Oxford...." He goes on to say that, though Crotch will only accept as valid the "pure sublime" style (that is, the sort of music exemplified by his own *Ten Anthems*), there are in fact five equally valid contemporary sacred styles: the Wesleyan school; the more dramatic style of Attwood and Novello; the "school adopted by those glee writers, who are not addicted to the schism propagated by the Oxford Professor, and which includes the names of Robert Cooke, Shield, Evans, Walmisley, Jolly and some others"; the S.S. Wesley style, "founded on a union of Purcell, Bach, and Beethoven"; and finally, *"the true sublime,* of which Messrs. Crotch and Horsley are pre-eminently the corner-stones".

Gauntlett accuses Crotch and Horsley of narrow-mindedness, of ignoring the most worthwhile developments in sacred music: "A dull canon, or a feeble imitation of Palestrina, will probably meet with greater encouragement"; and suggests that their method of adjudication "will ultimately effect a total change in our cathedral style of composition, and lead to its destruction rather than to its improvement." He further complains that Crotch and Horsley "write according to rule; but there is no sentiment—nothing varied, excellent, original, and racy. There is, in short, great industry but no genius....Dr Crotch, as a motett and glee writer, has written excellently; so also has Mr Horsley; but not one characteristic of their traits as composers appear in their church writings."

Although Crotch resigned as an adjudicator for the prize, he had still to contend with further adverse criticism, this time taking the form of accusations by Rimbault (also published in *The Musical World*) that musical examples in his three-volume *Specimens of various styles of music* were inaccurate, and therefore reflected upon Crotch's integrity as a scholar. He wrote, in 1842: ".... Dr Crotch's *Specimens* is a compilation of no authority; the whole of the compositions there printed having been derived from second-hand sources, frequently much corrupted. This is the more reprehensible on the doctor's part when we know that the magnificent libraries of Christ Church, and the music school, Oxford, were at his command, and had he shown a proper spirit of research, and a true regard for his name, by consulting them during the progress of his work, the *Specimens of various styles of music* might have been a work of some authority." In a private letter to his friend Callcott, Crotch replied to the attack by admitting that he preferred Arnold's adaptations of sixteenth-century Latin motets to the original versions in certain cases, and that they were of more use to an English cathedral choir. But he made no public reply; he seldom did.

Despite such attacks he remained a much-respected figure. Thus, in the same year that Gauntlett's invective was published in *The Musical World,* the same journal carried an article by Edward Hodges, which included the remark: "....the precocious development of the intellectual and imaginative powers is sometimes followed by a splendid career, through a long and well-spent life; and I am happy in being able to point to a *living* instance. The musical portion of the world, I am sure, will anticipate my naming DR CROTCH....". Complimentary reviews of newly-published compositions and editions of his works were also frequently to be seen in the musical press.

Once he had retired from public life, Dr Crotch became an almost legendary figure, a reminder of a past era; but this did not stop—indeed it positively encouraged young composers in their search for authoritative advice on their compositions. Crotch would charge a fee (whether he was approached privately or in his official capacity as Professor of Music at Oxford) for a usually courteous but discouraging opinion.

More revealing is the advice he gave on other topics. In reply to a letter from Samuel Sebastian Wesley (Samuel's natural son), he wrote on 30th December 1840: "....I consider an Organist bound to play the tunes appointed by the Clergyman tho' I regret that the latter should have anything to do with the music, tho' he ought to choose the words. When I was organist of Ch. Ch. I had frequently to play *Lord of all power and might* (Mason), a great favourite with the majority but a most contemptible production. I consider the tunes you mention as very objectionable but probably if that were respectfully submitted to your curate he would not appoint them again, even if he still continued to like them ....At all events we cannot *compel* anyone to have a musical taste or to *see that we have*—when they have not."

The performances at Miss Fryer's continued, the Club still met most weeks, pupils came to be taught. Friends and relatives visited, and when he was well enough, Crotch would call on them for dinner. He attended chapel as frequently as he could, though rarely with his wife, whose violent face-aches were recurring with growing regularity; when she was able, though, she attended missionary societies, one of which aimed to convert all Jews to Christianity.

Crotch continued his meteorological observations, and he became expert at making home-made fireworks. And all this time, he and his wife were comforted by a series of pet dogs. Following Gioco, they had owned Prince, who was unfortunately run over by a cart in 1838; then came Don, who died in 1843, an unnamed dog which had to be destroyed "for mischief", and finally Dash, who joined the household in April 1844.

On 6th September 1838, Crotch's great friend William Newbery died in Sussex, bequeathing to him all his paintings, drawings and prints, many of which were hung in places of honour when the Crotches moved down the road in August 1839, to number twenty-four, Bedford Place.

The elderly doctor (he was sixty-five in 1840 and looked older) visited Oxford for the last time in 1839, though as late as 1843 he was well enough for a stay in Brighton. Here, from his wheelchair, he admired the surf, drew scenes on the beach and had long conversations with a Mr Soule, whom he described as "a pious and pleasant dissenting Minister, but not averse to our church". When in London, he apparently loved "to be employed in making and painting toys for poor children who resided in the crowded quarters of Soho; and ....took care to have the little ones have access to him when his gifts were ready for disposal".

He also spent much time with his treasured library—his many theoretical books and papers, and his collection of old music.

But all this activity only disguised the fact that both Dr and Mrs Crotch were seriously ill. In addition to his leg trouble, which confined Crotch to bed for months at a time, a fresh cause for anxiety presented itself in March 1844. "A new complaint", he wrote in his *Memoirs,* "wch I do not know ye name of, a pain after breakfast near the collar bone and sometimes in ye shoulder, elbow and wrist; cordials named to relieve it." A year later, nose-bleeds, chest pains and more blisters on his leg, as well as a broken shin obtained when climbing out of a carriage.

Pride prevailed no longer. The elderly couple finally accepted their son's offer of a home under his roof in Taunton, where the old professor was in his element, surrounded by his son and grand-children, playing games with them and always telling them some new story. The fun reached its climax over Christmas 1847, and as his son said afterwards: "My father seemed for those few days to have a new fire". He apparently ate more than he had managed for some years.

Perhaps it was a result of the excitement—perhaps even because he ate too much; but whatever the reason, during dinner on the evening of 29th December, the old man had a sudden heart attack, though he remained sitting upright at table even after he had died.

The stone memorial tablet by the organ in the church of St Peter and St Paul, Bishop's Hull (a tiny village just outside Taunton) records:

> "His rare and various mental endowments, enhanced by the simplicity of his heart, and genuine humility, were all exercised in subservience to the principles of the Gospel of Christ; guided by which, he was enabled, through the Grace of God, to set his face against all evil, and to exhibit, in a life of remarkable serenity and happiness, though not without its periods of natural sorrow, the fruits of the Spirit, Love, Joy, Peace."

He was buried in the churchyard, beside his small grandson, Edmund.

CHAPTER ELEVEN

The Magic Influence
— Choral Music

THE quality of Crotch's musical compositions varies considerably from work to work. One finds peaks of inventiveness in, say, *Palestine;* but in contrast there are pages of instrumental and choral music neither ambitious nor particularly inspired, though rarely does one discover a bar whose technical craftsmanship is anything but impeccable.

Gauntlett's complaint that the *Ten Anthems* lacked sentiment, that they were the result of "great industry but no genius", has an element of truth, but fails to take into account their date of composition, the early 1790's when Crotch was organist of Christ Church, Oxford, and still in his late teens—which was, after all, a good fifteen years before he was writing his greatest music. A brief look at these eclectic pieces gives clues to Crotch's early influences, and shows the first few steps along the path which was to lead to *Palestine.*

It comes as little surprise to stumble upon *Amen* and *Hallelujah* choruses of the Handel school, as in the verse-anthem *Blessed is he:*

alongside chorus fugues of similar origin:

A verse from *The Lord, ev'n the most mighty* possesses a Purcellian flavour (in particular, the falling fourth at "Sion" to a rhythm approaching a "scotch snap", and the chromatically descending bass), and one wonders why Crotch's later music lacks reference to the "immortal Purcell", as he called him in his *Lectures:*

79

There are echoes of the chordal, hymn-type anthems of Thomas Attwood (1765–1838), Mozart's pupil and Crotch's friend, in *Comfort the soul of Thy servant* (the second half of *Be merciful*) —a favourite still with many choirs:

The full anthem *How dear are Thy counsels* (also still sung in many cathedrals) begins in similar fashion, but a modulation from E to major to F sharp minor (before moving on to B major) points the plea "try me, prove me", so imposing a climax on an otherwise mainly-diatonic movement.

The organ voluntary idiom of John Stanley (1713–1786) and William Boyce (1710–1779) is implied in the organ accompaniment to the *Rejoice greatly* section of the verse-anthem *Rejoice in the Lord:*

but in *Sing we merrily* the organ's trumpet stop is used more pictorially at the words "blow up the trumpet" (much as the harp is used in *Palestine* at "then the harp awoke"):

Here then, Crotch was recognisably feeling his way towards his mature style as manifested in *Palestine*. Once he had passed that point his choral works, with perhaps one exception, prove disappointing.

(xv)   Crotch watercolour. Field going out of Meadow Lane.   *Norfolk Record Office.*

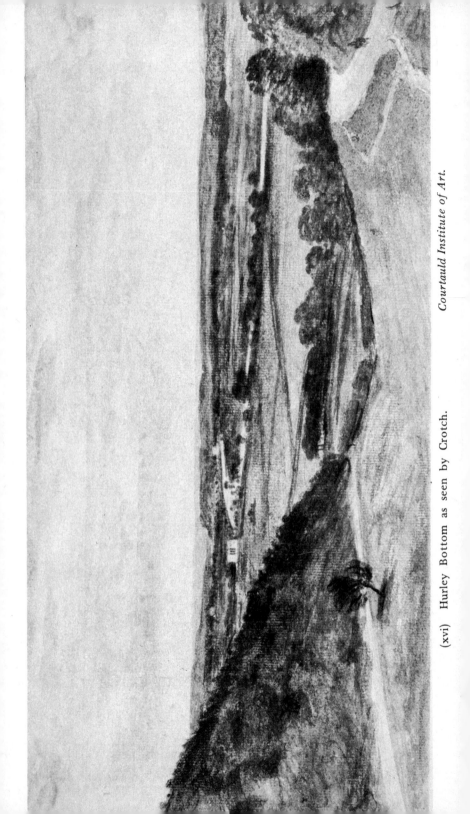

(xvi) Hurley Bottom as seen by Crotch.

Courtauld Institute of Art.

(xvii) Hurley Bottom as seen by John Constable.   *Victoria and Albert Museum*

(xviii) Kenilworth Castle by Crotch.

Ashmolean Museum, Oxford

(xix)   Kenilworth Castle by John Constable.   *Victoria and Albert Museum.*

(xx)   Crotch watercolour. Near the Fort, Brighton, 1834   *Norfolk Record Off*

(xxi)   Crotch watercolour. Two men and three children.   *Norfolk Record Off*

(xxii)   Crotch watercolour. Heathfield Park, Sussex 1811.   *Norfolk Museums Service.*

(xxiii) Illustration of Crotch's different handwritings.
Norfolk Record Office.

(xxiv) The headstone of Crotch's grave at Bishop's Hull.
The Author.

His third and last oratorio, *Captivity of Judah,* set to the same text as the earlier piece of the same name, received only two performances with complete chorus and orchestra—in Oxford on 10th June 1834 and at Vaughan's benefit concert at the Hanover Square Rooms on 16th May 1836. It was never published, even as a vocal score (though arias appeared individually), and was generally accepted to be a pale imitation of *Palestine.*

The work has in all probability never been heard as the composer intended, because of the perennial, but at that time acute, problem of lack of rehearsal. Thus after the London hearing, the critic of *The Musical World* remarked: "Much credit is due to all the parties engaged in the performance, seeing that they had not been able to give it more than one rehearsal; the choruses, there-fore, did not always go with that smoothness and decision which we could have wished; they wanted that variety of expression, which can be expected only form a practised knowledge of the sentiment of each phrase, as well as the mere phrase itself." The critic further censured a practice which was still common at the time: "Mr Knyvett both conducted and presided at the organ—a plurality of appointment which is incompatible with the well-going of such an orchestra". Similar complaints were in fact regularly levelled against the dual directorship of leader and conductor, and in 1844, when the pianist Buddeus played part of Chopin's first piano concerto with the Philharmonic Orchestra, *The Musical World* observed that he "was fettered by the discordant beatings of no less than three different individuals, viz.—Sir George Smart, who wielded the baton—Mr Loder, the leader of the evening —and Mr T. Cooke, *not* the leader of the evening. These gentlemen were all beating different times."

Captivity, then, was a failure with the public; and *Palestine* remained the most popular of Crotch's choral works. Two others which deserve a mention, however, are the "anthems" (or odes) *The Joy of our Heart is Ceased* (1827) and *The Lord is King* (1838; performed 1843).

The more formal of the two is the 1827 piece, written on the death of the Duke of York. It opens with an eight-bar *pianissimo* introduction for strings and tympani, after which the full orchestra (including three trombones, trumpets and clarinets) and chorus enter gradually, still *pianissimo:*

The work contains three large choruses and two treble solos, much of it at a low dynamic level and comparatively inhibited, to suit the occasion for which it was intended. In passing, it might be mentioned that the two clarinets (in C) are now spaced in the same way as the other woodwind instruments—no longer are they reserved for *tutti* passages and special solo effects.

On a more ambitious scale, *The Lord is King* was the last large-scale piece composed by Crotch. It is built in the following structure:

Number	Title	Category	Keys
1	(8-bar orchestral) Introduction		G
2	"The Lord is King"	Chorus	G
3	"The Heav'ns have declared"	Treble air	Bb
4	"Confounded be all they"	Chorus	c
5	"Worship him"	Chorus	C
6	"Sion heard of it and rejoic'd"	Treble Air and Chorus	C
7	"O Ye that love the Lord"	'Quintett'	E
8	"He shall deliver them"	Chorus (acting as a recit.)	g-e
9	"There is sprung up light"	Chorus	G-b
10	"Rejoice in the Lord"	SATB verse and Chorus	G

The mediant relationships between numbers create mounting excitement as they ascend from C major to E major to G major to B minor; indeed, in only two cases is the mediant idea not involved: between numbers 3 and 4, a quiet treble solo is followed abruptly by a loud, harsh chorus directed against them "that worship carved images, and that delight in vain" (the shift from the bright sound of B flat major to the darker C minor confirms the change of mood); and between numbers 4 and 5, the C minor of "delight in vain Gods" leads, quite conventionally, to the large C major chords of *Worship him*. This is not to say, though, that *Confounded* is without interest; it is cast in two halves, the first over a seven-times-repeated ground bass:

while the second is in seven-part canon (S.S.A.T.T.B.B.). The text forms verse seven of psalm 97, and one is tempted to suggest that this dwelling on the figure seven is no accident (though conclusive proof of Crotch's interest in number-symbolism is lacking).

The opening of the treble air *The Heav'ns have declar'd,* vacillating as it does between B flat major and G minor, shows perhaps-Schubertian traits:

At dramatic moments Crotch sometimes flattens the seventh, so that, in the opening chorus at the words "The earth saw it, and was afraid", a B flat major chord appears in a solidly C major passage, and the dynamic falls abruptly from *fortissimo* to *piano:*

A similar passage is equally dramatic in *Palestine,* in the chorus *Then the harp awoke*

though a bar using the same 'modal' procedure in *The Joy of our Heart* appears to have no especial dramatic significance, but just to be a useful cadence before the tenors embark on an imitative passage:

Crotch maintained that "music can awaken the affections by her magic influence, producing at her will . . . serenity, . . . ecstacy, melancholy, . . . terror, and distraction. She can remind us also of the sacred, military, and pastoral styles; and when poetry would speak of the thunder-storm, the battle, . . . the breath of the zephyr . . . or the merry peal of bells, music can by her imitations increase, almost infinitely, the enjoyment of the description." At first sight, these might have been the words of almost any of the nineteenth-century Romantic composers, and they serve to underline the trends already seen in Crotch's choral music. It is perhaps wise to disregard the fact that Crotch contradicted both this statement and much of his own practice by claiming that, as a descriptive art, music was limited to representing physical movement and action.

Crotch's most original music almost invariably resulted from the stimulus of a text. It is therefore in his music for voices that the "magic influence" of his art is most evident.

CHAPTER TWELVE

Organ Music

IN COMPARISON with Crotch's choral music, the solo organ
pieces are on a small scale, since their subdued, "sacred" style
was a conscious reaction against current trends in music for the
organ. Crotch complained: "The practice of organists shows that
'The praise and glory of God' is not so much thought of as their
own reputation for execution or invention. They perform on the
organ during divine service such pieces as are expressly composed
for the piano-forte, concert, or theatre; or pieces which do not
differ from them in style".

Crotch's organ music undoubtedly succeeds in avoiding the
most obvious secular fashions of the day, but the result is an
unhappy compromise between a show of academic skills (canon,
ground bass and fugue) in imitation of J. S. Bach, and a harmonic
vocabulary reminiscent of the piano sonatas of Beethoven, Hummel
and Clementi.

The *adagio* introduction to the *Fugue composed on a subject
of Theophilus Muffat's* (1806) draws much of its character from
suspensions and sequences just as does the *andante* of Clementi's
opus 50, no. 1:

The fugue, though, is a nondescript and conventional working.
Based on the subject:

it was composed when Crotch's knowledge of Bach's keyboard
music did not extend beyond the "forty-eight", and thus there is
none of the breadth of Bach's organ fugues.

The years 1835 and 1836 saw the publication of twelve fugues based on psalm chants, and presumably in an effort to attract more buyers, they are described as fugues "for the organ or piano forte"—a curious inconsistency for a man who advocated three entirely individual styles for the organ, the piano and the military band, and to give weight to his argument, pointed to the incongruity of "a military band on parade playing the soft adagios of Haydn, Mozart and Beethoven!"

An unsigned review in *The Musical World* (I, 2, p. 28) mentions the "lovely introduction" of number five (based on a chant by Norris) and says of the fugue itself: "the subject throughout is treated in a free and masterly manner; at the same time with a sweet and graceful feeling"; a comment which presumably refers to the chromatic movement, the sequential phrases and the quaver flow:

A number of these pieces end with a play-through of the subject (the chant), often preceded by a few bars over a dominant pedal, as in the twelfth of the set:

It is perhaps unfair, however, to judge Crotch (as a composer) on his music for solo organ, since the instrument had still not been fully developed in England by the 1830's, and although a number of organs could boast pedals and well-voiced choruses, they were mostly on a small scale, just as was the music written for them.

The three *organ concertos* are less limited in scope, the organ being joined by strings, flute and two horns (in the first), strings, flute, two trumpets and tympani (in the second), and in the third, by strings flutes, oboes, clarinets, bassoons, horns, trumpets, three trombones and tympani. They are in much the same style as the almost-contemporary organ concertos of Charles and Samuel Wesley, William Felton and "Mr Mudge", which in turn follow basically the example of Handel.

The conventional plan of the first two concertos can at once be appreciated from the layout of movements:

No. 1: Allegro (F); Andante (B flat); Allegro, Fugue (F)
No. 2: Allegro (A); Andante (E); Allegro, Fugue (A).

The unexpected occurs, however, in the third, whose B flat major *Allegro* is preceded by a thirteen-bar *Adagio* in B flat minor:

The *Allegro* itself begins, in *tutti* unison octaves, with a subject whose dotted minims and quavers prepare the listener for a contrapuntal approach:

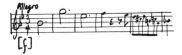

One is reminded of the *Finale* of Crotch's first organ concerto, and of the *Allegro* from Handel's F major concerto:

A new idea is heralded by the band, and the organ, which can either have the dual function of playing continuo during *tutti* passages and solo-work in the virtuoso organ-only sections, or can share these duties with a harpsichord, enters on its own:

The cadenza is written out in full.

The second movement (*Larghetto; piano e sostenuto*) is delicately scored; for example, a potentially "lumbering" melody is given poise by the addition (in bars 29 to 56) of a *pizzicato* violin line above the organ solo melody, an octave higher on the off-beat:

The fugue's sense of urgency is caused partly by its scurrying semiquavers, partly by a lack of harmonic complexity which aids its feeling of forward drive; but even here one finds chordal progressions which are far from naive, when one considers the date of composition (1804-1805):

The actual solo figuration in all three concertos tends to be fairly standardised, two of the most common devices being semiquaver and quaver-triplet passages; an example to prove this point also serves to demonstrate the close interrelation of styles between the concertos of Crotch and his contemporaries:

CHAPTER THIRTEEN

Crotch as Musician

THOUGH some of his compositions are very beautiful, he never made his own style or developed sufficient individuality to remove him from the crowd of second-rate composers whose works hardly outlive their own age". So said Heathcote Statham of Crotch in 1892.

Having considered the oratorio *Palestine,* the *Ten Anthems,* the anthems with orchestral accompaniment, the solo organ music and the organ concertos (a reasonably comprehensive cross-section of Crotch's music), one can make at least a tentative judgement of their worth, and of the value of the generally accepted, though ill-informed, view expressed by Statham.

Firstly, Crotch's English contemporaries respected him as a composer, teacher and organist with few rivals. Wesley referred to him as "among the most brilliant organists of our present day", adding: " . . . his great ability as a writer upon the scientific part of music is abundantly manifest in the treatises he has published on the subject—his oratorio of *Palestine* is a luminous evidence of his talents as a composer, as all those who have heard it must be ready to testify." He further called him "one of the most affable and candid men that exists".

Sterndale Bennett, arguably Crotch's most successful pupil, so admired his master's erudition that, when Mendelssohn was planning to visit England to do research on Handel, Bennett referred him to Crotch, saying that he was the only man in the country who truly knew and understood Handel's music.

With the occasional exception, contemporary musical journals were also complimentary. Thus in *Mainzer's Musical Times* (1st September, 1842), *Palestine* was described, a full thirty years after its first performance, as "one of the noblest works of the English school".

Today, two hundred years after his birth, it is easier to see Crotch in historical perspective—a perspective which demands comparison between him and that other, almost-contemporary prodigy, Mozart; a perspective which at once makes it clear that, though both performed astonishing feats as infants, their later childhoods and their adult lives differed radically. Mozart composed music which has unprotestingly survived two centuries of popularity, though he died young and was buried in a pauper's grave; Crotch settled down into a comfortable academic life, honoured by his contemporaries, dying in old age, but leaving to posterity only a comparatively small handful of musical compositions, most of them containing both fine craftsmanship and much originality—but little that could be called genius.

There were a number of causes, not the least of which concerns the two composers' early musical training. Mozart was given a thorough grounding in harmony and form, as well as in harpsichord technique, by his composer-father Leopold, which enabled him to write reasonably literate pieces by the time he was eight; Crotch, on the other hand, received no professional instruction until the age of eleven, thus wasting those vital years which could have been used to develop an extraordinary talent.

But Crotch could have made up for lost time even at this stage. In Cambridge he soon mastered the basic skills of a cathedral organist, and in Oxford he composed steadily, ever more competently. But somehow it never went further than that. Indeed after *Palestine* (1812) his horizons, instead of broadening, seemed actually to contract and, with only a few exceptions, he reverted to small-scale composition—to small organ fugues and psalm chants; even his teaching method as a Professor of Composition at the Royal Academy of Music came to be based on psalm chants.

It was a pity that English musical life gave Crotch no incentive to devote a larger portion of his time to musical composition. It would have been particularly fascinating to have seen him write more purely orchestral works, since the two symphonies and two overtures which he did produce show considerable understanding of orchestral colour, and they contain some unusual touches. But unlike his opposite numbers in Europe, and particularly the German court musicians who were required to produce a constant stream of new music, Crotch's only obligation as Oxford's Professor of Music was to write an occasional piece for a formal occasion. Furthermore, London audiences positively discouraged the performance of anything but music from the continent.

Thus Crotch was encouraged to spend more and more of his time in academic work, and as a scholar he figured in the forefront of those musicians dedicated to the revival of sixteenth-century music —as early as 1803 he produced editions of Tallis's *Litany* and the anthem *Come, holy ghost.*

Then as he grew older, his musical theories became more stubbornly inflexible, until on 4th March, 1833, he was writing in a letter: "The introduction of novelty, variety, contrast, expression, originality, etc., is the very cause of the decay so long apparent in our church music." This championing of the past to the absolute exclusion of the present was of course entirely misguided, and as Stainer pointed out: "Imitation of the past in music is a necessary process of pupilage; but to look upon it as an end in itself is surely destructive of all progress and expansion".

Fortunately the qualities of variety, contrast, expression and originality abound in Crotch's best music; and far from spelling decay, they demonstrate his strength as a composer. His ability to "break the rules" (for example, in *Palestine* or in the third organ concerto) proves that, though he felt no need to identify with a "Sturm und Drang" or any revolutionary cause—indeed, although on the surface he was very much a product of the Age of Reason, he was nevertheless not afraid to compose music of considerable impact; "Romantic" music, even though he could in no sense be seen as a Romantic hero-figure (a Beethoven, a Liszt or a Berlioz); music with great emotional appeal, even though the text he was setting might seem (to Schumann or Brahms) both dry and contrived.

Crotch's development as a composer was, then, curtailed by the harsh musical environment in England; and so were the careers of other promising young composers in the early nineteenth century (the Wesley brothers and Ouseley, for example). Perhaps they would all have done better to have left England. Crotch, on the other hand, fitted well into his surroundings—he never actually crossed the English Channel or the North Sea; his temperament might perhaps not have been suited to a life devoted exclusively to composing, without the addition of those interests which took so much of his time—drawing, his firework-making, his religious writings, his astronomical observations and his teaching. These were all necessary to him, and without them he might not have felt able to compose some of the best of his music, for which at least we should be grateful.

The professor was, in a sense, both feted and rejected simultaneously by his countrymen. He held the highest musical posts in the land, and yet audiences were indifferent to music from any mere Englishman. Little wonder that composing became a minor part of his life. Little wonder that his music was discarded immediately he died.

Only now can it be seen that the forgotten doctor, the wasted doctor, deserves reappraisal. Since he never fulfilled entirely his early promise, we can never know what exactly we lost. We must make do with what little music the English musical world allowed him to write. Some of it is worthy of any modern audience—or will these audiences behave just as did their ancestors? Will late-twentieth-century audiences despise his music, not so much because it was written by a fellow-countryman, but because the period in which Crotch lived is now unfashionable by definition? Or is it possible that Crotch might, at long last, be given a second chance?

Crotch as an Artist

CROTCH the musician spent many hours with pencil and paintbrush. When an infant he would continue with his chalking on the floor, in preference to playing the organ or harpsichord to inquisitive visitors; and as a child his drawing provided him with an escape from the unnatural life he was expected to lead. Many years later he remarked that he found drawing "a source of amusement, after the fatigue of professional duties", and that it had become such an essential part of his life that he could not decide "which I love best of these two sisters".

He was encouraged by artists both amateur and professional. In 1785 he met William (later Sir William) Beechey, who painted a full-length portrait of the ten-year-old sprawled on a large sofa, composing; and in Cambridge Crotch learned much from Mrs Peckhard, wife of the Dean of Carlisle and a friend of the boy's patron Jowett.

But his greatest encouragement came in Oxford from Johann Malchair who, besides leading the Music Room orchestra, was also a drawing master and the central figure in a movement sometimes called the Oxford School. Consisting of a few professionals but mainly of university undergraduates with an amateur interest in painting, the group preferred to be known as The Great School, with Malchair taking the role of "P.G.S.", or President of the Great School.

Members of this society later in life exercised the artistic judgement which they had acquired in Oxford, when they became wealthy patrons and collectors—as did, for example, Sir George Beaumont and a number of the aristocracy. This haphazard collection of art lovers has, indeed, been given credit for considerably influencing the fashions of taste in the art world for perhaps half a century.

But it has been further argued that Malchair's teachings found their most influential advocate, not in these well-known public figures, but in Oxford's Professor of Music, William Crotch, who passed on the old man's theories to someone who could put them to best advantage—John Constable.

Because of their mutual interest in both music and art, Malchair and Crotch became firm friends, and they discussed every possible aspect of Malchair's theories. When Crotch arrived in London, he met Constable (around 1806), and this friendship, too, soon developed. The link between the dying P.G.S. and the young professional artist was thus formed through an intermediary.

Crotch and Constable both came from the eastern counties, and although Crotch had not been brought up in the country, as Constable had, he was nevertheless strongly attracted to the small cottages and village churches, the cornfields and the oak trees, and the infinitely variable aspects of the sky, which formed the ever-recurring themes of both men's artistic work.

What exactly had Malchair taught Crotch? Certainly he had shown him some of the basic techniques of landscape composition, concentrating especially on aspects which might seem self-evident, but which can so easily be forgotten. Crotch was, as a start, taught to look for his subject; he gave an example later of the way he had learned to find the correct position in a field: "At first entrance the view struck me as good. I however remembered the constant advice of my good friend and able master Malchair, *always to walk about my subject before I began to draw.* I accordingly moved a few steps towards the N.W. and found the objects arranged much better. I was just going to begin my sketch but thought that it was not impossible that a few more steps to the right might still improve my view—which they accordingly did. Brill hills appeared in the distance in two points. Casting my eyes to the left I saw high trees which I thought would probably come in for a corner. A few steps more brought them in but they hid my pigeon house and part of the church tower—I stooped and they appeared!—I sat down and *drew!* Brother beginner—If thou hast *but* twenty minutes to spare—spend at least five in walking about your subject and take my word as well as Mr Malchair's you will not spend it in vain. Oh that I had taken this advice of my old Master's when at Battle Abbey! and a thousand times besides."

The pupil was grateful to his master for another piece of advice: "Forty different pictures are produced from the same subject in an hour", the old man had told him, when pointing out the constant variation of light and shade from one minute to the next. Crotch meticulously wrote on the back of many of his drawings the precise time of day, as well as the date and location of the subject.

Crotch learned from Malchair lessons which, to Constable, were instinctive. Here was the miller's son who had come to recognise every hovering cloud, every shudder of the corn, for the purely practical task of setting the mill's sails correctly; thus his younger brother is supposed to have said: "When I look at a mill by John, I see that it will go round".

What was it, then, that Constable was able to learn from the Great School? After all, he joined in 1806, at about the time Crotch took over as President, and there survive a number of sketches signed: "John Constable R.A., M.G.S.".

Probably both men found each other's capacity for experiment and discussion stimulating; for Constable, it came as a relief to forsake the standardised work expected by the public in favour of the style he had been privately developing, and which came to be appreciated by Crotch and his friends in the Great School; for Crotch, the association provided him with an opportunity to develop further his own artistic abilities.

The two men shared a liking for certain locations—Hampstead Heath and Brighton Beach both figure prominently in their work—and one finds a close similarity in treatment. The shimmering lights, the mists, the breeze-disturbed foliage, the swirling streams preoccupied both the amateur and the professional, and there are many appearances amongst Crotch's pictures of the effect known as "Constable's snow"—the illusion, caused by hundreds of tiny bare patches on the paper, of sparkling light; and Crotch mastered this technique with great effect in a number of portraits of trees.

Crotch always considered himself very much a novice in the art field, so that one finds many expressions of modesty on the backs of his drawings; for instance, "copy of Sir George Beaumont, 1802", "copied from a drawing by Mr Malchair, late P.G.S., 1805", "in the style of Mr Green of Bath", "N.B. Sir A. W. Callcott approved". Puns are also a common feature of these inscriptions; a sketch dated 10th December, 1838, is labelled: "In a new style or Payne's?—who can say I did not take pains; no—it is a new style".

Most of Crotch's watercolours (which are in fact pencil sketches with thin washes) are dated 1802-1842, though as early as 1789 he made his "first sketches from nature" in the Isle of Wight, and he sketched scenes in both Brighton and Budleigh Salterton in his last years. He occasionally painted in oils, but these works were generally rather formal and lacking in "atmosphere". There were also published a number of etchings by Crotch, of the ruins of a fire at Christ Church, Oxford (1809), of Holywell Mill, Oxford, and of Merton Fields, Oxford (both 1808).

Moreover Crotch wrote *A Treatise on Perspective* in 1842 (*Nro, ms. 11248*), and there exists a small sketchbook dated 1831 (*Nro, ms. 11068*) in which are contained elaborate notes and sketches describing the history of British architecture.

Crotch's artistic efforts could not be expected always to display the assurance of Constable's or Callcott's or Beechey's works; nor can one reasonably expect to find the consistency of style which would tend to mark the productions of professionals, especially since one of Crotch's greatest pleasures was to experiment in *different* styles.

What remains a surprise to many people is the high degree of competence which he attained, and which certainly classed him amongst the leading amateurs of his day. On the back of one of his sketches he wrote: "The Colisseum and ye Priory near Regent's Park. John Constable, R.A., told me he should be proud to own this as his sketch and desired me to write it here!" Perhaps one should not take this too literally.

However, Crotch cannot be written off as of no consequence whatever in the history of British painting. Whether considered as an influence on Constable or as a worthwhile artist in his own right, he merits a place in any account of the English art scene of the early nineteenth century.

Cath?	Reign	date	place	County	plates
11th	W^m II Rufus	1088 To 1123	Canterbury Transept / Lincoln Westfront	Kent page 30 / Linc.	1 36 61 116 121 126 134. 155 / 135 136 147 195. 194.
		1090	Margam ab.	Glamorg.	136.
		1091	Lindisfarne Priory	Durham	253
		1093	Durham Cath?	D.	24 86 96 114 123 124 135 138 139
		1095 to 1179	Hereford Cath. choir & nave	H.	141 142 166 167 191 192 / 76 102. 103 157
		1096.	Norwich Choir. Chapels Transepts Tower	Norfolk	13 43 58 190 36 59 60 61 146 62 63 64 65 66 67 68 69 70 11 72
		1096	Romsey Ch.	Hamps.	73 150 74 267 281
		1096	Carlisle Cath? Nave & South aisle.	Cumb?	40 41 ~~43 45 48~~ 104 attic bases
		1096	Ch. Ch. Priory nave	Hampsh.	81
		1097	Westminster Hall.	Mid.	no page 78.
	Henry I	1100	Gloucester nave	Glo.	58 59 61 63 64 65 66 67 68 69 70 71 72 73 74
			West front of Castle Rising ch.	Norpth	

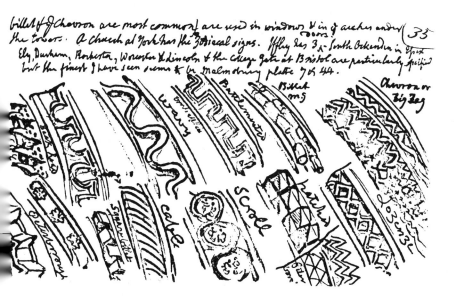

billet & of Chevron are most common & are used in windows & in of arches and of the towers. A Church at York has the Zodiacal signs. Iffley has 3 & South Ockendon in Essex Ely, Durham, Rochester, Worcester & Lincoln & the Cloister gate at Bristol are particularly specified but the finest I have seen seems to be in Malmesbury plate 7 & 44.

(35)

97

Catalogue of Musical Compositions

Holograph manuscripts are located by their RISM abbreviations and are printed in italics. In addition, to facilitate easy access to Crotch's music, the availability of printed editions of the major works in a few selected libraries and collections is denoted by the following numbering:

Number (printed editions)	RISM abbreviation (mss).	Library/Collection
1	*Lbm*	British Museum, London
2	*Nro*	Norfolk Record Office, Norwich
3	*T*	St Michael's College, Tenbury
4	*Lcm*	Royal College of Music, London (Parry Room)
5	*Lam*	Royal Academy of Music, London
6	*Lco*	Royal College of Organists, London
7	*Ob*	Bodleian Library, Oxford
8	*Och*	Christ Church, Oxford
9	*Ojc*	St John's College, Oxford
10	*Ouf*	Faculty of Music, Oxford University
11	*Cu*	University Library, Cambridge
12L	*Cjc*	St John's College, Cambridge (Library)
12M	-	ditto (Music society library)
13	*Cpl*	Faculty of Music, Cambridge University (Pendlebury library)
14	*Ascm*	Royal School of Church Music, Addington Palace
15	-	Property of Jonathan Rennert
16	*Lcml*	Central Music Library, London.
17	*Ckc*	King's College, Cambridge (Rowe Library)

In the catalogue below, other abbreviations are as follows:

acc.	accompaniment
arr.	arranged/adapted
c.	circa.
comp.	date of composition
d.	dedicated
ed.	edition
hpd.	harpsichord
incl.	including
instr.	instrumental

ms.	manuscript
orch.	orchestra(ted)
org.	organ
p.	date of first known performance
pb.	published/printed
pf.	pianoforte
repr.	reprinted
rev.	revised
sel.	selected
w.	words/text/libretto
v.	violin
vc.	'cello
vla.	viola

ORATORIOS (listed chronologically)

Captivity of Judah *(w. sel.* A.C. Schomberg and J. Owen), comp. 1786-9, *p.* Cambridge 4.6.1789; *Lbm, Add.* 30388

Palestine *(w. sel.* Crotch from Reginald Heber), *comp.* 1804-11, *p.* London 21.4.1812; *Lbm, Add 30390-1* (full score); *Ob, ms. 28972* (vocal score); T.ms. 1207 (full score, hand of J.C. Büdinger). Vocal score *pb.* 1812 (to be had of the author no. 2 Duchess Street...and Birchall's and Chappell's), plates marked *Palestine;* repr. 1818 (with list of Crotch's publications at North End, Fulham); repr. 1822-32(?)(by T. Welsh at the Royal Harmonic Institution) and 1822-32(?) (by Cramer, Addison and Beale). *2nd ed.* 1839 (Cramer Beale and Co.), plates numbered *2552,* G and F clefs only, same plates used by Novello. One or more of the above in 1, 2, 3, 4, 5, 6, 7, 8, 10, 11, 12M, 15. Octavo vocal score *pb.* 1879 (Novello), 1, 2, 3, 4, 5, 6, 7, 11, 13, 14, 15, 16, 17. See also under *Anthems.*

Captivity of Judah *(w. sel.* A.C. Schomberg and J. Owen), *comp.* 1812-28. *p.* Oxford 10.6.1834; *Lbm, Add.* 30389, *Nro, ms. 11260; T.* ms. 330 (hand of J.C. Büdinger). See also under *Anthems.*

OTHER WORKS FOR CHORUS (SOLOISTS) AND ORCHESTRA

Part of Messiah, a Sacred Eclogue, cantata *(w.* Pope), *comp.* 1790; *Lbm, Add.* 30392

Chorus to Humanity *(w. sel.* Crotch from W. Mason's *Elfrida), comp.* 1790-91; *Lbm, Add. 30392*

O Sing unto the Lord, anthem *(w.* from psalm 96), *comp.* 1794 as exercise for MusBac; *Ob, ms. 26872, p.* Oxford 28.5.1796

Ode to Fancy *(w.* J. Warton), *comp.* 1799 as exercise for MusDoc, *p.* Oxford 21.11.1799; *Ob, ms. 26874.* Full score *pb. c.* 1799-1800; (Broderip and Wilkinson), 4, 5, 8, 11

Ode for the Installation of Lord Grenville as Chancellor of the University of Oxford, *comp.* 1810; 10

Ode on the King's Accession *(Spirit of the golden lyre) (w.* J.J. Conybeare), *comp.* 1820, *p.* Oxford 1821; *Lbm, Add.* 30396

Hail Sympathy, glee and chorus, with instrumental accompaniments composed for the anniversary of the Royal Society of Musicians, *comp. ?(before 1824). Pb.* Robert Birchall), 4, 8.

The Joy of our heart is ceased, anthem, composed on death of his Royal Highness the late Duke of York, *comp. and p.* 1827; *Nro. ms. 11270.* Full score *pb.* 1827 (Royal Harmonic Institution), 5, 6, 8

Ode for the Installation of the Duke of Wellington as Chancellor of the University of Oxford *(When these are days of old) (w.* J. Keble), *comp.* 1834, *p.* Oxford 11.6.1834; *Lbm, add. 30389.* Extracts (3 airs: *Then onward, Day of stern joy, Warrior, be such our course and thine) pb.* 1834 (Oxford, for the author), 1, 7, 8, 11

The Bells, *comp.* 1836, *p.* (privately) 7.4.1836, public performance (planned for 27.4.1836) "given up for want of bells"; *Nro, ms. 11275*

The Lord is King, full anthem *(w.* from psalm 97), *comp.* 1838, *p.* London 10.3.1843; *ms. lost?* Vocal score *pb.* 1843 (J. Surman; also Novello), 1, 4, 6, 8, 10, also *pb.* (1843?) string parts, wind parts and vocal parts.

O give thanks, full anthem, *comp. ? Lbm, add. 30395*

Choruses and uncompleted choral items in *Lbm, add. 30392*

SERVICE MUSIC

Te Deum in Bb, *comp.* 1790; *Lbm, add. 30392*
Gloria Patri, canon 2 in 1. *Pb.* 1831 (Harmonicon)
Kyrie in F. *Pb.* 1844 (R. Fawcett. *Lyra Ecclesiastica)*

ANTHEMS (listed alphabetically)

Ten Anthems, "respectfully dedicated (by permission) to the Dean and Chapter of Christ Church, and composed for the use of that cathedral." *Pb.* 1798, *2nd ed.* 1804 (revised by the author). One or more of the above in 1, 2, 3, 4, 6, 8, 9, 10, 11, 13, 14. Anthems from this collection are marked * below; those published by Novello (ed. Monk), 1856-61, are marked +. Many of the latter also appeared in the Novello Octavo series.

Be merciful unto me *+ *(w.* psalm 86), *comp.* 1794; *Och, ms. 1226.* An excerpt, *Comfort the soul of Thy servant,* later *pb.* with altered text: Comfort, O Lord, the soul of Thy servant: 1886 (Novello Octavo)(this version *repr.* in *Form of Service for the Centenary Celebration of the Royal Academy of Music,* 17.7.1922; 1937 (York, Banks and Son); 1954 (Curwen/Schirmer); 1969 (OUP, arr. female voices)

Blessed is he whose unrighteousness is forgiven* *(w.* psalm 32)

Entomed here doth by a worthy wyght (Epitaph on the gravestone of Tallis), *comp.* 1799; *T, mss. 599*

God is our hope and strength *(w.* psalm 46), 1st version; *Lbm, add. 30392*
God is our hope and strength *(w.* psalm 46), 2nd version; *Och, ms. 1226*
How dear are Thy counsels *+ *(w.* psalm 139), *comp.* 1796; *Och, ms. 1226;* 1880, Parish Anthems Book (Boosey)

Hymn to the Trinity *(Holy, holy, holy) (w.* Reginald Heber), *comp.* 1827. *Pb.* 1859 (Addison and Hodson); *c.* 1876 (The Singer's Library, part 7)

I acknowledge, motett, *comp.* 1801, *T, ms. 600*
I have nourished, motett, *comp.* 1802; *T, ms. 600*
In God's word will I rejoice, *comp.* ? (mentioned in letter dated 24.6.1838). *Pb.* (Cramer, Addison and Beale/Novello)

Judah mourneth the gates thereof, motett, *comp.* 1798; *T, ms. 599*

Methinks I hear the full celestial choir, glee/motett/madrigal (*w.* 'from Thomson'), 1st version, *comp.* 1796; *T, ms. 598.* 2nd version, *comp. 1800, p.* 24.9.1800, *p.* (with orch.) 19.4.1819; *T, ms. 600. Pb.* 1800 (Broderip and Wilkinson); *c.* 1815 (Preston); *c.* 1819 (with instrumental accompaniments) (Regent's Harmonic Institution); *c.* 1820 (Royal Harmonic Institution); 1838 (Cramer, Addison and Beale); 1851 (Novello Octavo); 1926 (Bayley and Ferguson); 1937 (Schirmer, N.Y.); 1972 (Roberton)

My God, my God, look upon me *+ (*w.* psalm 22)

O come hither and hearken, *pb.* (Cramer Addison and Beale/Novello); 1907 (Novello Octavo)

O let my, motett, *comp.* 1799; *T, ms. 599*

O Lord Almighty God, 'glee', *comp.* 1798; *T, ms. 599*

O Lord, from whom all good things do come, *comp.* 1800; *T, ms. 600. Pb.* 1825 (*A. Pettet: An Original Collection of Sacred Music*)

O Lord God of Hosts *+ (*w.* psalm 84); *Och, ms. 1226*

O Lord, we beseech Thee, motett, *comp.* 1800; *T, ms. 600*

Out of the depths, motett, *comp.* 1799; *T, ms. 599*

Rejoice in the Lord, O ye righteous* (*w.* psalm 33). An excerpt, *Behold, thy King cometh,* later *pb.* separately

Righteous art Thou, motett, *comp.* 1798; *T, ms. 599*

Sing we merrily*+ (*w.* psalm 81), *comp.* 1794 (for Christmas Day); *Och, ms. 1226*

The hour of prayer (*Not only at the hour of prayer, O Lord*), hymn; *pb.* (Willis and Co., Royal Musical Library), 8.

The Lord, ev'n the most mighty God, hath spoken* (*w.* psalm 50)

Trust ye in the Lord, motett, *comp.* 1798; *T, ms. 599*

Who is like unto Thee, O Lord God of Hosts *+ (*w.* psalm 89)

The following numbers from *Palestine* were published individually:

Be peace on earth, quartet and chorus; *pb.* 1874 (Lonsdale); *c.* 1880 (Ashdown and Parry); 1898 (Novello); 1937 (York, Banks and Son, York Series 437); 1949 (arr. S.S.A.) (York Series 1504)

But now thy sons, air and chorus; *pb.* 1874 (Lonsdale)

But who shall dare recite, recit., and Awe-struck I cease, air; *pb.* 1874 (Lonsdale)

In frantic converse, air and semichorus; *pb.* 1874 (Lonsdale)

Is this thy place, sad city, recit., and Ye guardian saints, air; *pb.* 1874 (Lonsdale)

Lo! star-led chiefs; *Lam; pb.* in arrangements for S.A.T.B.: (Novello Octavo); 1937 (York Series 436); 1965 (*arr.* 2-part) (Oxford Easy Anthems); 1966 (*arr.* S.S.A.) (Chappell)

Such, the faint echo, duet; *pb.* 1874 (Lonsdale)

The following numbers from the second setting of *Captivity of Judah* were published individually:

Israel is a scattered sheep, recit., and But he shall feed on Carmel, air; *pb.* 1836 (R. Mills)

Oh, that my head were waters, duet; *pb.* 1836 (R. Mills)

HYMN TUNES AND PSALM CHANTS

Many ms. and printed collections contain hymns and, particularly, chants by Crotch. A large number of his essays in this genre are to be found in the following:

Psalm tunes selected for the use of cathedrals and parish churches, *pb.* 1836 (London); New ed. (ed. Elvey) for voices and org., *pb.* 1843 (London)

A collection of 72 original single and double chants (*ed.* Crotch), *pb.* 1842 (London)

The national psalmist, *pb.* 1842 (London)

Ms. sources, apart from chant books compiled for the use of individual cathedrals and collegiate chapels, include the following in Crotch's hand:
Lbm, Add. 30392; Nro, mss. 5288, 11234; Och, 1143, 1226
See also: *Works edited,* under *Tallis, Litany*

SECULAR VOCAL MUSIC (listed chronologically)

Those pieces marked * were printed by Robert Birchall (1st. edition, 1806; 2nd. edition, *c.* 1820); those marked ** by the Royal Harmonic Institution (*c.* 1810); those marked + by Lonsdale (*c.* 1868-74):

Liberty, a new song composed by Master William Crotch; *pb.* 1786 (Holland & Co.), 6

Sycamore Vale (*w.* Miss Garland of Norwich), *comp.* 1787; see: Crotch's *Memoirs,* p. 56

A rose had been washed (*w.* Miss Hawkins), *comp. c.* 1787

Clear shines the sky,* canzonet, inscr. Miss Pears, for solo voice & accompaniment of pf. 'or harp'; *pb.* before 1824, 1,8

Hail all the dear delights—on returning to Heathfield Park,*** glee (*w.* F. Newbery); *pb.* before 1824

The Academy Roll Call to Dinner, round (*w.* Crotch, incl. puns on names of his pupils), *comp.* 1826; *Lam*

Like as the damask rose you see, glee (*w.* Simon Wastell); *pb. c.* 1840(?) (R. Mills)

Yield thee to pleasure, old care,* glee (*w.* R. Bloomfield); *pb.* 1892 (Novello)

The following are grouped separately from the preceding items because they are all to be found in the three volumes of the Harmonic Society of Oxford (*T, mss. 598/599/600*):

	comp.	
Hence, Bacchus, glee	24.8.1796	*T, ms. 598*
O, be favourable, canon	31.8.1796	,,
If aught of oaten stop, glee (ode to evening)	12.9.1796	,,
For ever fortune, glee	6.10.1796	,,
What sounds divine, glee	27.10.1796	,,
Hallelujah, canon	8.11.1796	,,
At parting, round	1.12.1796	,,
Yet mighty God, glee	17.12.1796	,,
O sing unto the Lord a new song, canon	4.1.1797	,,

God be merciful, canon	12.1.1797	"
To love thee, O my Emma sure*, glee, *p*. London 17.4.1801	19.1.1797	"
Hallelujah, canon	26.1.1797	"
Nymph with thee at early dawn—address to health*, glee	18.2.1797	"
Pietas omnium virtutem, round	March 1797	"
Let thy loving mercy, round	26.4.1797	*T, ms. 599*
O come, let us sing, canon	21.5.1797	"
Lord, what love have I, round	1.6.1797	"
Ὦ ὄρακνα, round	4.6.1797	"
In Domino confido, glee	11.6.1797	"
O how sweet, canon	28.6.1797	"
Go, tuneful bird*, glee	15.8.1797	"
Amen, round	20.9.1797	"
I will always, canon	10.10.1797	"
God is the Lord indeed, canon	12.10.1797	"
Hear me, O Lord, canon	20.10.1797	"
O Lord, my help, contrapunto	21.10.1797	"
Weep no more (answer to Lycidas), glee	22.10.1797	"
Ring out, ye crystal spheres, glee	6.11.1797	"
Soft is the strain, glee	8.11.1797	"
Ye woods and wilds, glee	22.11.1797	"
Why hast thou cast us out, round	15.12.1797	"
Sing we merrily, round	3.1.1798	"
Amen, round	30.1.1798	"
Why hast thou, round	6.2.1798	"
Howl, O Israel, canon	28.3.1798	"
O sing praises, round	31.3.1798	"
Call forth such numbers, glee	16.4.1798	"
Mona on Snowdon calls*** (ode from Mason's *Caractacus*), glee	24.4.1798	"
Bow down thine ear, canon	26.5.1798	"
Go lovely rose, round	16.6.1798	"
Why so disquieted, round	22.9.1798	"
Wee modest crimson tipped flow'r, glee	1.10.1798	"
For ever blessed, canon	15.10.1798	"
O Lord, grant the King, canon	23.10.1798	"
Gloria Patri, canon	5.11.1798	"
O Music, round	23.2.1799	"
On Harmony (Laetitiae comes), 8-voice round	2.3.1799	"
Turn then, canon	March 1799	"
My heart is ready, canon	March 1799	"
O sing praises, canon	"	"
Let's have a round, round	"	"
Bimbim, bembem, bambam/All the bells, round	"	"
I will alway, round	May 1799	"
O be joyful, canon	June 1799	"

Ponder my words, canon	”	”
Great art thou, round	July 1799	”
Blessed art the dead, canon	August 1799	”
Lord, let me know, canon	September 1799	”
Te benedicimus, canon	October 1799	”
Lord unto Thee, canon	”	”
Amen, canon	”	”
When the wicked moan, canon	”	”
Lord, hear our prayer, canon	”	”
Lord, Thou hast heard, canon	”	”
O sing praises, canon	November 1799	”
When music, glee	”	”
Holy Lord God, canon	”	”
Deus nobis, round	December 1799	”
Amen, round	January 1800	”
Stabat mater, round	February 1800	”
Hallelujah, round	March 1800	”
Quis est homo, serious round	April 1800	”
See, urged to wrath, serious glee	May 1800	”
Hallelujah, round	July 1800	*T, ms. 600*
Hear, O Heavens, canon	August 1800	”
Why hast thou, round	September 1800	”
Praise the Lord, canon	October 1800	”
Blessed be the peace-makers, round	November 1800	”
Hallelujah, round	February 1801	”
Ponder my words, round	March 1801	”
Woe unto us, canon	”	”
Hallelujah, round	12.4.1802	”
My compliments present, catch	12.4.1802	”
Snowdon, glee	February 1803	”
Welcome to our genial hearth, glee	December 1803	”
Painter's Lingo—founded on faith ('As the fam'd Sir George B. and his friend Sir George A. were bowling along in a rattle post chay'), round	December 1803(?)	”
As parting Emma shed a tear, round	June 1803(?)	”
Che non è dolce, round	September 1806	”
Sweet sylvan scenes—on leaving Heathfield Park** (*w.* F. Newbery), 5-voice glee, adapted from 4-voice version of September 1807. Also *Glasgow University (Euing Collection)*	24.2.1808	”
One, two, three, four, five (All Saints' bells, Oxford), round	26.11.1818	”
Death, thou wert once a hideous sight, serious glee	30.1.1823	”

ORCHESTRAL MUSIC AND CONCERTOS
(listed chronologically)

Concerto, hpd. or pf., 'with an accompaniment for 2 violins and bass' (*d.* Burney by 'Master Crotch, the self-taught musical child, aged 9 years'), *comp. c.* 1784, *p.* London 27.5.1785; *Nro, ms. 11246. Pb.* 1785 (Holland), 8

Overture in A, *comp.* 1795; *Lbm, Add. 30393*

Concerto, org., no. 1 in F, *comp. c.* 1804-5, *p.* London May 1805; *Nro, ms. 11250.* Score *pb. c.* 1805 (Birchall), 1,2,6; orch. parts *pb. c.* 1805 (Birchall), 2

Concerto, org., no. 2 in A, *comp. c.* 1804-5; *Nro, ms. 11250.* Score *pb. c.* 1805 (Birchall), 1,2,6,7; orch. parts *pb. c.* 1805 (Birchall), 1,2,7

Concerto, org., no. 3 in Bb, *comp. c.* 1804-5, *p.* Oxford 25.6.1805; *Nro, ms. 11274.* Score *pb. c.* 1805 (Birchall), 1,2,6,7; orch. parts *pb. c.* 1805 (Birchall), 2,7

Sinfonia no. 2 in Eb, *comp.* 1808, *rev.* 1817; *Lbm, Add. 30394.* Pf. duet arrangement *pb. c.* 1819 (Regent's Harmonic Institution), 3,5,7,11

Overture in G, *comp.* 1815; *Lbm, Add. 30393* (together with orch. parts)

Sinfonia in F, *comp.* 1814-15, *p.* London 16.5.1814 (or 1815?); *Lbm, Add. 30393.* Pf. duet arrangement *pb. c.* 1819, 3

CHAMBER AND KEYBOARD MUSIC (listed chronologically)

Various juvenile compositions are in ms. notebooks in *Nro*

2 Sonatas, pf. or hpd., *pb. c.* 1786 (London); see: Crotch's *Memoirs,* page 51

Quartet, strings, *comp.* 1788, *rev.* 1790; *Lbm, Add 30392*

3 Sonatas, pf. or hpd., in A, D, Eb, *pb. c.* 1794 (J. Bland), 3,6,7,8,11

Sonata, pf., in G, *comp.* 1795; *Lbm, Add 30392*

Original airs in various and familiar styles, pf., by John & William Crotch, *pb. c.* 1800 (for the author), 6,11

Prelude & Air, pf., in E, *pb. c.* 1806 (Birchall), 4,6,7,8,11

Milton Oysters, or Yeo, yeo, pf., 'inscribed to the lovers of imitation, fugue, canon, inversion, diminution, augmentation, & c.', *pb. c.* 1806 (Birchall), 7 (Och, ms. 1191 is a printed copy annotated by Crotch)

Fugue of a subject of Theophilus Muffat's, org. or pf., *pb.* 1806 (Birchall)

Sonata, pf., in Eb, *pb.* 1808 (Birchall)

Preludes for pf.; see: *Theoretical Works*

Fantasia, pf., *pb.* (before 1824) (Birchall), 8

3 Divertimentos, pf., *pb. c.* 1825 (Royal Harmonic Institution); no. 1 in 1 (imperfect), 8; no. 2 in 8; no known copy of no. 3

March & Waltz, pf., *Nro, ms. 11234.* Orch. version *p.* at the Private Concerts of Her Majesty the Queen, 1832; orch. score *pb.* 1832, 8,11. Pf. duet arrangement *pb.* 1833 (Lonsdale & Mills)

Fugue on a subject of 3 notes, org. or pf., *pb. c.* 1825 (Royal Harmonic Institution)

Introduction & Fugue, pf. or org., in F, *pb. c.* 1825 (Royal Harmonic Institution), 8

12 Fugues, the subjects taken from chants, org. or pf., *pb.* 1835-1837 (R. Mills); nos. 1-12 in 6,8; nos. 1-2 & 7-10 in 7; nos. 1-2 & 7-12 in 11; no. 1 in 1:

no. 1 in F: subject from double chant by Revd. P. Henley, 1760

no. 2 in E: subject from chant by Battishill

no. 3 in A minor: subject from chant by Battishill

no. 4 in A minor/major: subject from chant by Soper

no. 5 in F: subject from chant 'by T. Norris' [actually by Dr Philip Hayes]

no. 6 in A minor: subject from old chant, author unknown

no. 7 in C: subject from chant by Jones, Organist of St Paul's

no. 8 in F: subject from chant by Dr Hayes, Professor of Music, Oxford

no. 9 in D: subject from part of chant by Dr P. Hayes, late Professor of Music, Oxford

no. 10 in E minor: subject from chant by Revd. W. R. Crotch

no. 11 in A: subject from chant by Dr Blow

no. 12 in C: subject from old chant, author unknown

(n.b.: no. 5, ed. with added pedals by West, *pb.* 1905 as no. 10 in *Old English Organ Music,* 11)

(n.b.: *Andantino in C* in *The English Organist,* book 1, is an arrangement of the last bars of overture to *Palestine,* arr. Orlando A. Mansfield; *pb.* 1932, Paxton)

WORKS EDITED, COMPILED OR ARRANGED BY CROTCH

(listed in alphabetical order of original composers; dates refer to publication; arrangements are for pf. solo or pf. duet unless otherwise stated)

Beethoven, Symphony no. 6, arr. pf. 'with accompaniments for violin & violoncello', 1858

Cimarosa, Finale to Act I of *Il Matrimonio Segreto* (Royal Harmonic Institution)

Corelli, 'First Concerto' (Royal Harmonic Institution)

Crotch, March & Waltz; see: *Orchestral Music*

Crotch, from *Palestine,* 'the overture, quartetts, sestett and choruses', *c.* 1830; 8

Crotch, 2 Sinfonias; see: *Orchestral Music*

Dussek, *The Ploughboy*

Francalanza, Collection of Italian & French canzonets, *pf. acc.* Crotch, *c.* 1815

Galliard, *The Hymn of Adam and Eve, pf. acc.* Crotch, 1847 (Novello's Cheap Musical Classics, vol. 53)

Geminiani, Concerto [grosso, op. 3, no. 1], *c.* 1819 (Antient Relics for the Piano Forte, no. 4)

Gibbons, Te Deum & Benedictus (from Service in F), *instr. acc.* Crotch, *p.* Oxford 25.6.1805; ms. score/parts lost?

Greene, *Sing unto the Lord,* anthem

Handel, the works of (Handel Society); vol. 1.: Anthems for the coronation of King George II., ed. Crotch, 1843

Handel, Selections (overtures, choruses, marches, sinfonias, etc.) *arr.* from many oratorios and choral works, including: *Alexander's Feast, Messiah, Saul, Ode for St Cecilia's Day, Esther, Deborah, Athalia, Acis & Galatea, Dryden's ode 'From Harmony', Israel in Egypt, L'Allegro ed il Penseroso, Saul, Samson, Semele, Belshazzar, Susanna, Hercules, Occasional Oratorio, Joseph, Judas Maccabæus, Joshua, Alexander Balus, Solomon, Dettingen Te Deum*

Handel, 'Six hautboy concertos'

Haydn, String quartet in C (*'Bird'*), 'Haydn's favorite quartet', *c.* 1811.

Haydn, String quartet in E (op. 2, no. 2), [also] 'Haydn's favourite quartett', *c.* 1812

Haydn, 12 Sinfonias, arr. pf. 'with accompaniments for the violin and violoncello' (Royal Harmonic Institution)

Haydn, Sinfonias (nos. 7,8,10 of Salomon's set)

Haydn, A selection of Sinfonias, *c.* 1826

Kozeluch, 'Celebrated Sinfonia', *c.* 1825

Meyerbeer, from *Il crociato in Egitto,* 'Coro dello Sbarco' & 'Giovinetto Cavalier', *c.* 1826 (Royal Harmonic Institution)

Mozart, *Cosi fan tutti, Una bella serenata, Fortunato l'uom che prende, c.* 1818 (Rutter & McCarthy)

Mozart, *Don Giovanni;* arr. include pf. & v. or flute, pf. & flute, pf. duet:

Mozart, from *La Clemenza di Tito,* overture & finale, arr. pf. duet
  i) on a new plan (3s. 6d.)
  ii) arranged in the usual way (4/-)

Mozart, from *Die Zauberflöte,* overture (Royal Harmonic Institution)

Mozart, Sinfonia in C ('Jupiter') (Royal Harmonic Institution)

Mozart, 'Concertos nos. 1-3'

Mozart/Zelehner, 'Mozart's 12th. Mass', four subjects selected from (actually Zulehner's Mass in G), *c.* 1840 (R. Mills)

Nehrlich, Air with variations

Pergolesi, Gloria in excelsis Deo

Romberg, Overture in D

Rossini, 'Cruda Sorte'

Tallis, *Litany* (adapted to the Latin words with additions by Dr Aldrich), together with *A collection of old psalm tunes adapted to the old and new version for the use of the University Church, Oxford* and Tallis's *Come Holy Ghost* ('performed at ordinations'), 1803 (printed for the editor)

Weber, from *Der Freischütz,* finale

Other arrangements by Crotch include:

Chappell's *Collection of national English airs, harm. Crotch & others* (London, 1838-40)

The Old Hundredth ('The 100th Psalm, old version'), orch. Crotch, 15.9.1808; *Ascm, unnumbered ms.;* also a version *p.* Oxford Music Meeting, June 1805

THEORETICAL AND LITERARY WORKS
(listed alphabetically)

Elements of musical composition, comprehending the rule of thorough bass, and the theory of tuning, 1812 (Longman); *2nd. ed.* 1833 (Longman); *3rd. ed.* 1857 (Novello's library for the diffusion of musical knowledge); 1,3,5,11,16

Lectures on the history and theory of music, 1806-1832, 11 vols., *Nro, mss. 11063-67, 11228-33*

Preludes for the piano forte, 1822 (Royal Harmonic Institution), incl. *Rudiments of playing the pianoforte;* 6 incomplete, 8,11

Practical thorough bass, *c.* 1825 (Royal Harmonic Institution/Welsh & Hawes); 6,11; 8 has Crotch's own corrections

Questions for the examination of pupils who are studying the works called
'Elements of musical composition', 1830 (Royal Harmonic Institution)
Rules for chanting the psalms, 1842 (R. Mills)
Specimens of various styles of music 'referred to in a course of lectures, read
at Oxford & London, and adapted to keyed instruments', 3 vols. &
Appendix, 1808 (Birchall); *2nd. ed. c.* 1822 (Royal Harmonic
Institution); *3rd. ed. c.* 1845 ('with corrections & additions') (Cramer,
Addison & Beale). Complete or incomplete sets in 1,2,3,4,5,6,7,8,11,
13,14,16. (Also: O. Mansfield: *Mélodie Russe,* from *Specimens* vol. 1,
arr. pf., *pb.* 1934)
Substance of several courses of lectures on music, read in the University of
Oxford, & in the Metropolis, 1831 (A. & R. Spottiswoode); 1,3,5,11,15

In addition to the above volumes, there are extant plays (including a comedy
in 3 acts written by Crotch at the age of six, with music, illustrations
and dialogue, entitled *Robin Goodfellow or Fairy Lane*—now in the
New York Public Library's Berg Collection). Crotch wrote on subjects
as diverse as architecture, anatomy, astronomy, bellringing, botany,
chemistry, electricity, fencing, fortifications, geometry, physics,
Christianity, etc. Articles which he contributed to journals also cover a
wide range of subjects.

DRAWINGS AND PAINTINGS

A large collection of Crotch's paintings, drawings and etchings is in the
possession of *Nro,* and there are sketch books at *Lam.* A number of
private individuals specialise in the collection of Crotch's watercolours.
A list of some of these is kept at *Lam,* and the William Crotch Society is
in contact with others.

Bibliography and Discography

BOOKS

Bennett, J. R. Sterndale: *The life of William Sterndale Bennett* (Cambridge, 1907)

Bumpus, John S.: *A History of English Cathedral Music, 1549-1889* (London, 1908)

Busby, Thomas: *Concert Room and Orchestra Anecdotes of Music and Musicians*, III (London, 1825)

Busby, Thomas: *A General History of Music from the Earliest Times to the Present, p.* 520 (London 1819)

Corder, Frederick: *A History of the Royal Academy of Music* (London, 1922)

Curwen, J. Spencer: *Studies in Worship Music*, 1st. series (London, 1880)

Done, Agnes E.: *A Short Account of our great Church Musicians, 1540-1876, specially written for choristers* (London, 1903)

Douglas, Winfred: *Church Music in History and Practice* (London, 1962)

Elvey, Lady: *Life and Reminiscences of George J. Elvey* (London, 1894)

Fellowes, Edmund (Rev. Westrup): *English Cathedral Music* (London, 1941; rev. 1969)

Glover, William: *The Memoirs of a Cambridge Chorister* (London, 1885)

Grove, G.: *Dictionary of Music and Musicians*, 1st. edition (London, 1883), under 'Specimens'

Havergal, Rev. W. H.: *Psalmody and a Century of Chants* (London, 1870), 'Prefatory & Supplemental Notes'

Huntley, G. F. (ed. F. J. Crowest): *English Music, 1604-1904* (London, 1906)

Joyce, F. W.: *The Life of the Rev. Sir F. A. G. Ouseley, Bart.* (London, 1896)

King, A. Hyatt: *Some British Collectors of Music* (Cambridge, 1963)

Kitto, Armand W.: *William Crotch and his vocal works* (PhD diss., Washington Univ., 1967)

Knowles, Atherton: *Text-book of Anglican Service-Music* (London, 1895)

Lloyd, C. H.: *Lecture on Dr Crotch—his life and works* (delivered in Oxford, 1892; Ch.ch.ms. 511)

Lonsdale, Roger: *Dr Charles Burney* (Oxford, 1965)

Maitland, J. A. Fuller: *English Music in the XIXth Century* (London, 1902)

Naumann, Emil: *History of Music*, trans. Praeger, ed. Ouseley (London, 1886)

Parry, W. H.: *Thirteen Centuries of English Church Music* (London, 1946)

Phillips, C. Henry: *The Singing Church* (London, 1945)

Rainbow, B.: *The Choral Revival in the Anglican Church, 1839-72* (London, 1970)

Routley, Erik: *The Musical Wesleys* (London, 1968)

Sainsbury, John H.: *A Dictionary of Musicians* (London, 1824)

Smith, W. J.: *Five Centuries of Cambridge Musicians* (Cambridge, 1964)

Stainer, Sir John: *The Character and Influence of the late Sir Frederick Ouseley* (Proceedings of the Musical Association, 1890)

Statham, H. Heathcote: *My Thoughts on Music and Musicians* (London, 1892)

Temperley, Nicholas: *Instrumental Music in England, 1800-50* (PhD diss., Cambridge Univ., 1959)

Wainwright, David: *The Piano Makers* (London, 1975)

Walker, Ernest: *A History of Music in England* (Oxford, 1907)

Young, Percy: *A History of British Music* (London, 1967)

Wesley, S. S.: *A Few Words on Cathedral Music* (1849, reprinted London, 1965)

NEWSPAPERS, JOURNALS AND PERIODICALS

Charles Burney: *Account of an Infant Musician* (Philosophical Transactions of the Royal Society, lxix, 1779)

Daines Barrington: *Some Account of Little Crotch* (Miscellanies, London, 1781)

Articles, reviews and mentions in *The Quarterly Musical Magazine and Review:* I: 108, 130, 228, 478 (1818); III: 108, 279 (1821); IV: 370-400 (1822); VI: 170 (1824)

Memoir of Dr Crotch (*European Magazine*, 1822)

Review of *Preludes for the Pianoforte* (*Harmonicon*, 1823, 27)

Crotch's Lectures (*Harmonicon*, 1823, 88; 1824, 123; 1829, 160)

Review of *Palestine* (*Harmonicon*, 1827, 206)

Review of performance of *Palestine* (*Harmonicon*, 1828, 92)

Reminiscences of Oxford by Oxford Men (Oxford Historical Soc., vol. 22)

Review of *Palestine* (*Quarterly Musical Magazine*, I, 478)

Review of *Captivity of Judah* (*Monthly Supplement to the Musical Library* III, 1836, 94)

Articles, reviews and mentions in *The Musical World:* incl. I: 28, 78, 79, 113, 158-9, 163; II: 81, 97, 113, 146, 187 (1836)

W. Gardiner (*Music and Friends*, I, 1838, 33)

Correspondence partly concerning the scholarship of Crotch's *Specimens* (*Musical World*, letters 4.11.1842 & 15.11.1842) answered by Crotch in a private letter to Callcott.

Dr Rimbault: *Musical Precocity* (*The Musical Standard*, 2.9.1876)

William H. Cummings: *William Crotch, Mus. Doc.* (1889)

Letter suggesting erection of gravestone at Bishop's Hull (*Musical News*, 5.6.1897)

G. M. Garrett: *The Choral Services in Chapel* [of St John's College, Cambridge] (*The Eagle*, XVI, 224-9)

John S. Bumpus: *The Compositions of Dr Crotch* (*Musical News*, XIII, 371, 396)

The Organ Recital (*Musical Times*, XL, 1899, 601)

T. W. Taphouse & F. Cunningham Woods: *John Malchair—A Forgotten Worthy* (publ.?; copy in Ch.ch.ms. 511)

Hilda Barron: *William Crotch, Musician and Painter* (*Country Life*, CIII, 2663, pp. 230-1, 30.1.1948)

C. L. Cudworth: *The English Organ Concerto* (*The Score*, no. 8, September 1953)

M. Raeburn: *Dr Burney, Mozart and Crotch* (*Musical Times*, XCVII, 1956, 519-20)

P. F. Williams: *J. S. Bach and English Organ Music* (*Music & Letters*, XLIV, 1963, 140-51)

I. Fleming-Williams: *Dr William Crotch, Member of the Oxford School and Friend of Constable (The Connoisseur*, CLIX, May 1965)

Stanley Sadie: Review of performance of *Palestine* (*The Times*, 26.2.1973)

Anthony Hicks: Review of performance of *Palestine* (*Financial Times*, 26.2.1973)

Robin Langley: Review of performance of *Palestine* (*Musical Times*, April 1973, 409)

Rodney Tibbs: *Wait a minim—who was Crotch?* (*Cambridge Evening News*, 19.10.1973) (launching of William Crotch Society)

Other short announcements about the William Crotch Society have appeared as follows:

Musical Times, December 1973, 1226

Musical Opinion, October 1973

Organ Club Journal, November 1973

Promoting Church Music, January 1974

Cambridge Evening News, 8.2.1974

Dolmetsch Foundation *Bulletin*, September 1974, 19

(Cambridge) *Varsity Handbook*, 1974-5, 179

Musical Opinion, March 1975, 309, 329

DISCOGRAPHY

At 1st January 1975, only two gramophone records containing music by Crotch were available:

LPB 663 (Abbey): *Lo! Star-led chiefs* (from *Palestine*), arranged for full choir and organ. Choir of Liverpool Cathedral; Noel Rawsthorne (organ).

SQUAD 111 (Qualiton/Decca): *Lo! Star-led chiefs* (from *Palestine*), arranged for full choir and organ; *How dear are Thy counsels* (from *Ten Anthems*). Choir of Brecon Cathedral; David Gedge (conductor), Hazel Davies (organ).

The William Crotch Society

Following the revival of Crotch's oratorio *Palestine* in the Chapel of St John's College, Cambridge (23rd February, 1973), the William Crotch Society was formed "to promote the performance and publication of Dr Crotch's music, and to encourage research into all aspects of his work."

The committee of the Society was as follows:

Charles Cudworth	(President)
Jonathan Rennert	(Secretary)
Robert Wallbank	(Treasurer)
Janet Buckley	(Archivist)
and Philip Booth.	

The inaugural committee meeting took place in Cambridge on 23rd July, 1973, and many Crotch enthusiasts have since joined the Society.

Index

A
Abel, Carl, 22.
Aberdeen, 19, 21.
Arnold, Samuel, 52, 76.
Ashby de la Zouch, 22.
Attwood, Thomas, 37, 65, 75, 80.
Avison, Charles, 27.
Ayr, 19.

B
Bach, John Christian, 16, 59.
Bach, J. S., 16, 43-6, 50, 75, 85.
Bangor, 37.
Barnett, 72.
Bartleman, James, 49, 52.
Basildon, 25.
Bath, 34, 72.
Batten, 72.
Bayswater Chapel, 72, 77.
Beadon, Dr, 29.
Beale, William, 37.
Beaumont, Sir George, 93, 95.
Beckwith, John, 40.
Beechey, Sir William, 93, 96.
Beethoven, 46, 72, 75, 85, 86, 91.
Bennett, Sir William Sterndale, 43, 65-6, 89.
Birmingham, 19.
Bishop's Hull, 78.
Bishop of Norwich, 73.
Bishop, Sir Henry, 65.
Blacklock, Dr, 20.
Blagrove, Henry, 66.
Bliss, Martha (Mrs Crotch), 35, 40, 41, 51, 64, 77, 78.
Bliss, Mr (sen.), 34.
Bliss, Robert, 33, 34.
Blow, John, 49.
Bochsa, 66.
Boyce, William, 47, 80.
Brighton, 77, 95, 96.
Broadwood's, 41.
Brodie, Sir Benjamin, 73.
Brunswick, Duke of, 63.
Buckingham, Marquis of, 49.
Burghersh, Lord (later Lord Westmorland), 65, 67-8.

Burney, Dr Charles, 13, 14, 16, 22, 27, 37, 38, 71.
Burney, Mrs, 27.
Bury St Edmunds, 15, 18.
Byrd, William, 43.

C
Caldwell, Captain, 72.
Callcott, John, 37, 41, 76.
Cambridge, 15, 18, Ch 3, 32, 41, 52, 63, 90;
  —Corpus Christi College, 28, 31;
  —Emmanuel College, 29;
  —Gonville and Caius College, 29;
  —Great St Mary's, 28;
  —Jesus College, 29;
  —King's College, 28, 29, 31;
  —Magdalene College, 29;
  —Petty Cury, 29;
  —Queens' College, 29;
  —St John's College, 28, 29;
  —Shoemaker Row, 28;
  —Sidney Sussex College, 28, 29;
  —Trinity College, 28, 29, 37;
  —Trinity Hall, 29, 33.
Cambridge, Duke of, 63.
Captivity of Judah, 30, 33, 43, 72, 81.
Carlisle, 19, 21, 29.
Chapel Royal, 27, 65.
Cherubini, 46.
Chester, 19, 20.
Chichester, 64, 72.
Childe, William, 72.
Clarence, Duke of, 63.
Clementi, Muzio, 24, 29, 44, 65, 85.
Club, the, 72, 77.
Colchester, 30.
Constable, John, 63, 94-6.
Cooke, Benjamin, 21, 31.
Cooke, Robert, 75.
Corelli, 44.
Corfe, Dr, 43.
Cramer, Wilhelm, 16.
Crane, James, 28.
Croft, William, 72.

Potter, Cipriani, 37, 65.
Pring, Isaac, 49.
Pring, Joseph, 37.
Purcell, Henry, 45, 72, 75, 79.
Pye, Kellow, 75.

Q
Quarterly Musical Magazine & Review, 52, 57.

R
Rameau, 27.
Randall, Dr John, 15, 27-9, 49, 54.
Raphael, 46.
Reading, 24.
Reynolds, Sir Joshua, 34, 43, 47.
Richmond, 70.
Rimbault, 76.
Ripon, 19.
Roberts, 32.
Routh, Dr, 40.
Royal Academy of Music, 37, Ch 9, 70, 75, 90.
Royal Institution, 50, 70.
Rugby School, 22.
Russell, 52.

S
Salisbury, 72.
Salomon, 29, 34, 50.
Sandhurst, 63.
Sarti, 66.
Saville, Sir George, 22.
Scarlatti, 44.
Schomberg, Rev. A. G., 22-6, 27-8, 30-1, 33-4, 71.
Schubert, 83.
Shakespeare, 26, 27.
Sharpe, Jonathan, 28.
Sheffield, 19.
Shield, William, 65, 75.
Sidmouth, 72.
Skinner, John, 35.
Slatten, Mr, 34.
Smalley, 72.
Smart, Sir George, 52, 65, 81.

Specimens of Various Styles of Music, 39, 44-6, 76.
Stainer, Sir John, 43, 91.
Stanley, John, 18, 80.
Statham, Heathcote, 89.
Stevens, Richard, 74.
Stowe, 49.
Sudbury, 18.
Surrey Chapel, 64.
Surrey Institution, 63.

T
Tallis, Thomas, 38, 91.
Taunton, 72, 73, 78.
Ten Anthems, 75, 79-80, 89.
Thetford, 15, 18.
Twining, Rev. Thomas, 30.
Tye, 44.

V
Vaughan, 81.
Viotti, 66.
Virgil, 26, 34.

W
Wakefield, 19.
Walmisley, T. A., 75.
Walmsley T. T., 28.
Ware, 15, 18.
Webb, Mr, 39.
Weber, 46, 66.
Wesley, Charles, 18, 25, 32, 87, 91.
Wesley, Samuel, 18, 19, 25, 27, 34, 45, 50, 63-4, 74-5, 87, 89, 91.
Wesley, S. S., 75, 76.
Wilberforce, William, 28.
William IV, 16.
Willins, Mr, 29.
Winchester, 48, 71.
Worcester, 19, 52.

Y
York, 19, 20.
York, Duke of, 63.

Z
Zingarelli, 66.